The GRIT in the OYSTER

THE BIOGRAPHY OF JOHN BURTON

First Edition

First published in November 2003 by The Northern Echo, Priestgate,
Darlington, County Durham DL1 1NF. The Northern Echo is part of
Newsquest (North East) Ltd which is a Gannett company
Website: www.thisisthenortheast.co.uk

Picture credits
Front cover picture by Raoul Dixon of North News and Pictures, Newcastle,
taken at Trimdon Labour Club on election night, 2001
Picture of the Sedgefield Supergroup by Keith Taylor (and may not be
reproduced without the photographer's express permission)
Back cover picture: Tony and Cherie Blair and John Burton celebrate winning
the Sedgefield seat in 1987 (from The Northern Echo archive)

A CIP catalogue record for this book is available from the British Library

ISBN 0-9540518-9-0

Printed by Northumbria University, Newcastle

The GRIT in the OYSTER
THE BIOGRAPHY OF JOHN BURTON

by Keith Proud

Edited by Chris Lloyd

Foreword by the Right Honourable
Tony Blair MP

The Northern Echo

The author
Keith Proud was born and brought up in County Durham and educated at Wolsingham Grammar School in Weardale from 1957-64. He then went to Durham to train as a teacher at the College of the Venerable Bede. In the late 1960s, while still in his first teaching post, he began to work at weekends for one of the first of the then new local radio stations, BBC Radio Durham. His long association as both presenter and producer with the BBC lasted for more than 30 years, during which time he made radio programmes in Scandinavia, Cyprus, Austria and the Falkland Islands. In 1987 he won a prestigious Sony Award for the Best Radio Outside Broadcast of that year. He has been writing since 1970, almost invariably about the history and people of the North-East England. Since 1989 he has taught at Macmillan College, Middlesbrough

The editor
Chris Lloyd is the political editor and assistant editor of The Northern Echo, the regional morning newspaper for North-East England which is Sedgefield's local newspaper

The cause
Trimdon Village Hall, a registered charity, is a popular meeting place for people of all ages in John Burton's home village. Situated near the new library and the local shops, it has served the community for some 40 years. But in 2003, it began showing signs of its age and major rebuilding work is now required. For each book sold, £1 will be donated to the rebuilding fund.

Contents

Acknowledgements

THERE are so many people to whom I owe many thanks for their assistance in the writing and preparation of this book.

Heading the list must be John Burton himself, along with his wife Lily, for affording me the privilege of telling this story at all. John, Lily and their children gave so generously of their precious free time to answer all of the countless questions I put to them over a period of some three years.

I had first put the idea for this book to John at Trimdon Labour Club on Election Night 1997 when I was covering the proceedings as part of my role at the BBC; he initially rejected it on the grounds that nobody would be interested, he believed, in his biography. It was almost two years afterwards that he decided that he did, perhaps, have something of a story to tell, and that, maybe, somebody might be interested enough to read it.

I want to record my most sincere thanks to Tony Blair, the Prime Minister, for so kindly writing the foreword to this book and for his numerous invaluable and candid contributions to its content.

Hilary Armstrong, Peter Mandelson and Mo Mowlam also gave freely of their time to share their memories of the impact John Burton made on their lives and times.

To Lord Dormand of Easington, I owe special thanks for his contribution to this volume and for the fact that he so kindly loaned me a copy of Danny Webster's brilliant History of the College of the Venerable Bede, the mere existence of which I was completely unaware.

Neil Kinnock was unstinting in his praise of John Burton as one of the originators of New Labour. He took immense trouble, in his hectic schedule, to share his memories of John and of Burton's part in the creation of the political revolution which subsequently became New Labour. It is to Neil that I also owe the title of this book.

The staff of those in and about Myrobella, in Trimdon, have made the business of writing this book much simpler than it might have been. They have also been more than generous in their provision of innumerable cups of coffee, plates of biscuits and sandwiches. To Christine, Rita and Mick, many thanks.

I also want to thank all the contributors of photographs, whose work has helped to illustrate this book. Many of the pictures are from The Northern Echo's archives. I must also thank North News and Pictures for allowing Raoul Dixon's picture of Tony and John on stage at Trimdon Labour Club on the night of the 2001 General Election to grace the front cover. Keith Taylor has also made available two splendid photographs – including, for the first time, one of the Sedgefield Supergroup.

At The Northern Echo, and its parent company Newsquest (North East), I need to thank the managing director David Kelly and the editor Peter Barron for so enthusiastically taking up this project. I am also very grateful to Petra Stanton for designing the cover, and to Richard Simpson for the lay-out and all the technical tomfoolery. The book was published at Northumbria University in Newcastle for which I have Andrew White to thank.

As ever in such ventures, there are many to whom I owe a debt of gratitude which is not acknowledged here, essentially those who encouraged me to write this book. To all of you, many thanks.

My wife Barbara's support and encouragement have been invaluable.

Finally, I want to thank most sincerely my editor Chris Lloyd of The Northern Echo, not only for his superb work but also for having had the foresight to see that this was a worthwhile project which deserved to be brought to fruition and for making that possible. Without his contribution, this book might never have seen the light of day.

Chris – thank you very much indeed.

Keith Proud
Eaglescliffe
October 2003

John Burton: The Grit in the Oyster

PRINTED AND PUBLISHED
BY THE NORTH OF ENGLAND
NEWSPAPER CO., LTD., AT
—— THEIR WORKS IN ——
PRIESTGATE, DARLINGTON.

Foreword by Tony Blair

I OWE many people, not least the voters of Sedgefield, a debt of gratitude for my political career, but no one deserves my thanks more than John Burton. Without him, it must be doubtful whether I would ever have become Prime Minister.

He was the first person I saw in Sedgefield. It was in his home that first night that I met the handful of people who convinced the local party to take a chance on me as their Parliamentary candidate. I moved into John's house to fight the campaign and have never since, I suppose, left his life.

My debt of gratitude to John, of course, goes far beyond that first meeting and election campaign. He's been a good and loyal friend, a constant source of wise advice with the sense of humour and fun to raise anyone's spirits. John is someone you always look forward to meeting.

He has also remained the staunchest of political allies and, as my Parliamentary assistant and agent, he's been my eyes and ears within the constituency. He's known – and liked – by everyone in Sedgefield and across the region.

But I also owe him a big debt for the role he has played in helping modernise our party – vital for our historic electoral success. I don't know what John and the other members of the 'Famous Five' saw in me when I turned up in Sedgefield in 1983. But I believe that part of the reason they agreed to support me was that they recognised someone who shared their vision for the constituency and the wider party.

John and his friends already understood that our party must modernise to reflect better the needs and ambitions of the people who depended upon us to improve their lives. John Burton is living proof that New Labour had its roots solidly in the traditional Labour area of the North-East. It's why many of the reforms which helped our party win back the trust of the country were piloted here in Sedgefield under his guidance.

So this book is not just the story of the remarkable and worthwhile life so far of a good and decent man. It is also, in its way, a story of how our party successfully made the decisions needed to win us the chance we now have to change our country.

Tony Blair

Introduction: And thereby hangs a tale

WHEN, like Tony Blair, you are Prime Minister of Great Britain, everybody wants to know you, everybody wants you to do something for them, everyone wants you to solve their problems.

When, like Tony Blair in 1983, you are nothing more than a young barrister who is wanting to become a Member of Parliament, patrons, allies and even political friends tend to be exceedingly thin on the ground.

As the run-up to the 1983 General Election gained momentum, Blair's time and options were running out. He needed all the allies he could muster. Almost every Constituency Labour Party in the land had selected its candidate; the newly-created Sedgefield seat in County Durham was one of the few that had yet to do so.

There were a lot of runners in the field for this safe seat. At the eleventh hour, with every other door closing in his face, Blair decided to throw his cap into the ring.

He made a telephone call to John Burton, a local Labour councillor who was secretary of the Trimdon Village branch – one of a handful of branches which had not yet put up a candidate.

"Would Trimdon Village be interested in nominating me?" the young London barrister asked the local Labour secretary. "And if so, could we meet as soon as possible to talk things through?"

The rest is history; Blair was selected and elected, and the chief architect of both these coups was John Burton. The full story of Burton's life, of how he came to be the right person in the right place at the right time to help to engineer a political and social revolution and of his on-going support for, and friendship with Tony Blair after 1983, has never before been told. This is that story, the tale of a man who helped to change history.

The politics of John Burton are an open book. Even before Blair came onto the scene, Burton was challenging the national Labour Party's ethos.

"Why," he asked, "are there, comparatively, so few members of the party?"

"Why," he challenged, "is it necessary for prospective party faithfuls to be members of a trade union? Why are they required to pay a fixed annual membership fee? Suppose them to be unemployed and on their beam ends; why should that be a barrier to membership? Surely it's better to have willing, active members than sustain former, virtually-lapsed ones who fulfil the criteria of the rule book but fail to support us in the way we need them to."

Burton and a few friends set about recruiting new party members in Trimdon Village by telling them that they did not have to be members of a trade union in order to become members of the Labour Party but that they could, subsequently, apply to join one should they wish to do so. Burton argued that union-to-party was not a one-way street; it would be quite natural for some to go the other way, from party to union.

Burton's unorthodox bending of the rule book incurred the displeasure, even the anger, of Labour politicians both locally and nationally. But his course was set and would prove to be highly successful.

Burton is one of the staunchest supporters of Tony Blair's New Labour philosophy. Indeed, Burton was probably New Labour before Blair, and he certainly helped show Blair how the old party needed to change.

Hilary Armstrong, MP for neighbouring North West Durham and Government Chief Whip, points out: "Everybody keeps saying that New Labour is a metropolitan invention but those of us in the North-East know that it is very far from that. In the early 1980s, a number of us, notably John, were saying openly that 'Old Labour' had had its day. A radical rethink, a complete modernisation, was necessary, indeed inevitable, but getting people to listen was incredibly difficult.

"Old Labour was male-dominated, clannish and a bit exclusive. It was totally out of touch with ordinary members of the public. It was not raving left-wing, it was simply stuck in a belief that the world was still as it had been 40 or 50 years previously. It was cosy. You could blame the Tories for anything and everything.

"What was needed was a grass-roots mass party with a lot more members and John persuaded Tony that this could be done. He had himself already proved that it could be!"

In contrast to another MP in another neighbouring seat who toiled in the background to create New Labour, the Financial Times has dubbed Burton "Labour's Prince of Light".

His physical trademarks are his pipe, a ready smile, his large moustache, a shock of greying hair and a characteristic, gently-ambling gait. He looks for all the world like a northern farmer but is, in fact, a retired teacher who still believes passionately that not only should young people be educated in such a way that they are employable when they leave school but that they must be equipped to push forward the enterprise culture, able to create jobs and prosperity for themselves and for others.

Well-liked, honest, self-effacing, generous (especially with his time), kind, outgoing, avuncular, prepared to listen to all sides, intensely loyal, determined, approachable and possessed of the most wicked sense of humour, he is, above all, shrewd. He is no man's fool. He is also famed as a raconteur, a man who tells a good story and who tells it well. Burton is always an excellent companion.

13

John Burton: The Grit in the Oyster

Anyone trying to understand what drives John Burton, the close confidant and mentor of Prime Minister Blair for nearly 20 years, needs only look at some words which he first read many years ago. In 1934, Henry Agard Wallace, the American politician and writer who became Franklin D Roosevelt's Vice-President during the Second World War, wrote: "I've always believed that if you envision [envisage] something that hasn't been, that can be, and bring it into being, that is a tremendously worthwhile thing to do.

"Our utopias are the blueprints of our future civilisation, and as such, airy structures though they are, they really play a bigger part in the progress of man than our more material structures of brick and steel. The habit of building utopias shows to a degree whether our race is made up of dull-spirited bipeds or whether it is made up of men who want to enjoy the full savouring of existence that comes only when they feel themselves working with the forces of nature to remake the world nearer to their heart's desire.

"We must invent, build and put to work new social machinery."

Wallace also made another astute statement which was to help to clarify the young Burton's political ideas. He said: "Parties are of value only insofar as they make it possible to put into action certain principles of social justice."

Burton was not even born when Wallace was philosophising, but as he grew up in Trimdon Village he took the American's words on board and eventually became a local politician who would go on to help to spearhead and engineer one of the greatest political revolutions of the late 20th Century.

Like any biography, however, this is not simply the tale of one person's life; no biography can be that. Every life, great or small, is comparable to a single thread which runs hither and thither through a tapestry made up of thousands of such strands interwoven into a common canvas. During a lifetime, like the tapestry thread, every man and woman deliberately or inadvertently touches the lives of countless others. Few set out to do so but all follow the age-old pattern; some merely brushing the existences of their fellow men, others, like John Burton, leaving an indelible mark.

There is no doubt that Donald Burton, his father, was a significant influence on John's life. Both attended the same teacher-training college, both became teachers and were, in turn, secretary to the local church council, son succeeding father and John serving in that capacity for 23 years until life became too hectic for him with all his other responsibilities. He continues to be a member of that same Trimdon church council, is still a churchwarden there and serves on both the Deanery and Diocesan Synods.

When he was just 15, he was interviewed about entering the Church of England priesthood by Canon Stranks at his home in the College – the name given to that great, tranquil quadrangle with its long green, to the south of Durham Cathedral. Six years later, an eight-year-old called Anthony Charles Lynton Blair would attend Durham Cathedral Chorister School, tucked away in a corner of the College.

Burton's meeting with the great churchman was a success and it was agreed that he would proceed towards taking holy orders, but, through a variety of circumstances, he never did.

He feels very strongly that some decisions in his life appear to have been made for him as if guiding him along a pre-ordained path. There are those, he readily concedes, who will scoff at such a notion; others may call it fate or pure coincidence but he firmly believes that his life has been directed by a greater force. "You can call it the hand of God, if you like," he says. "Call it what you will."

He has never been a Bible basher, hammering his beliefs at others but, as a Christian, he firmly believes that there is, beyond any shadow of doubt, what might be called "a grand design", that everyone comes into this world for a reason, to do a job, just one, and that none of us knows when we have served God's purpose.

He recalls, modestly, that he was the youngest ever Football Association coach, full badge, when he was in his mid-twenties. He did a lot of work for the FA but did not take his interest as far as he could have done, considering that soccer was, at the time, the great love of his life. His father insisted that he needed a "proper job – with qualifications".

His proper job turned out to be as a teacher, which caused him to move away from his native North-East to Hertfordshire. Despite all the attractions down south, he soon returned to his roots so that his wife Lily could have their first child in hospital – there had been no hospital beds available near them in Hertfordshire.

The Burtons settled in Stockton-on-Tees but it was not to be a long stay. John, now the grown-up son, was just getting to know his father really well as an adult, going out for a pint with him and enjoying seeing him come along to support him at football matches, when this strongest of relationships came to an abrupt and tragic end. Donald Burton was only 57 when he died of cancer.

John had altered course, then, four times, or his course had been steered for him: away from the Church, away from major football, away from a comfortable job far from "the grim north", and back to Trimdon Village.

"It was as if the place was a magnet and yet I never, even once, thought that at the time," he says.

This book is, in part, an account of one of history's most unlikely yet most

15

successful partnerships; Tony Blair and John Burton are two men from totally different backgrounds, brought together by fate, chance or some other, greater, force.

Ultimately, they were to try to catch a rainbow, to pursue what frequently appeared to be the seemingly unattainable goal of creating a modern, user-friendly Labour Party which would be eminently electable and would go on to win two huge landslide victories, paving the way for it to complete two successive terms in office for the first time in its 100 year history.

Burton says: "Very few people gave us a snowball's chance in Hell of achieving our aims. The difference between them and us was that we were convinced that there had to be just a few snowballs around in Hell and, like those snowballs, we didn't mind the heat – well, not a lot!"

One of the most telling tributes to John Burton is by the former leader of the Labour Party, Neil Kinnock, now Vice-President of the European Commission. In so many ways, his words fit perfectly into this introduction to Burton's story: "Oysters, by themselves, are merely a shell with some primitive life inside. To make a pearl, they need some grit.

"The same is true of voluntary organisations – and specially true of the Labour Party. There are values, convictions in each branch, in each constituency. But the triumph of ideals has to be organised. If there aren't a few people convening, collecting, campaigning, cajoling, conscripting – yes, and sometimes conspiring in the cause too – then the party becomes little more than a figure of political speech. There's little vision and even less vigour.

"Those people are the hardcore. If they didn't exist, many others who are well-intentioned but less eager would lead more peaceful lives – but representation would be weaker; democracy would go limp.

"However, there's a danger too.

"If the comrades become an introverted clique, selfishness sets in. It can sometimes take the form of sectarianism or jobbery. Incest is as damaging in politics as it is in any other sphere. 'Activism' becomes a sort of exclusive religion and people who anoint themselves 'activists' become a kind of druidic order. Life becomes an endless round of caucusing by people who have nothing in their lives but politicking. The party loses touch because the community – local or national – has become nothing more than an electorate; the voters have become 'punters'. The idealism dies. There's just the shell – with some primitive life inside.

"John Burton is grit. Indeed, he's probably one of the flintiest particles that the party has ever had. And the reason is that, for him, political activity is not an end in itself – it's a way of getting things done.

"That's common amongst the grit element in the Labour Party. In John's case, life is about music, sport, friends, having a laugh – and trying to make the best things in life available for everyone. That's where his politics come from. There are lots of people of all political beliefs and of no political beliefs who would quite like their fellow men and women to have security and care and opportunity – but not to the extent that they want to do very much about it. John Burton and people like him don't think that the needs of the age allow them to be so passive. Desiring progress is a sharp spur, not just a nice idea. For them, activism is a verb, not a noun and politics is outward-looking, never introverted,

"This doesn't make such people secular saints. If they were, they'd be insufferable. It's simply that their own enjoyment of living increases when there's more justice, more chances, more serenity in the neighbourhood, the nation, the world. Their value to the party and to society doesn't come from their purity; it comes from their normality.

"Of course, not everyone is John Burton. Not everyone had the wit or lack of reverence for convention and rules to say to people: 'Join the Labour Party and pay what you can afford – when you can afford it.' Not everyone seems to approach just about every problem by saying: 'We've got to do something about that.' Most prefer: 'You've got to do something about that.'

"Not everyone has a similarly-motivated bunch of men and women to share the actions, second the motion, make the argument; real political pearls, after all, need more than just one piece of grit.

"Not everyone's talent-spotting extends to sponsoring a future Prime Minister, especially when, given a slight twist of fate, a little more ambition and a little less generosity, a respected, articulate local teacher aged 43 might just have thought of securing the Sedgefield Parliamentary candidature for himself.

"Maybe John Burton is lucky to have all of these attributes. Maybe it's more than luck. Maybe it's energy and persistence, sweat and guts. Background might have something to do with it; but everybody has a background. What has always made, and makes, John special is that he had and continues to have a foreground – objectives to be reached, a better future to be built.

"All of this contributes to making John Burton a pleasure to know, not just because of what he is but also because of what he typifies. Two underused words describe him and men and women like him: enlightened and emancipated. The best thing about John and his kind is that they want to spread both understanding and freedom around and they are willing to work to do so.

"When Tony Blair was obviously going to be elected leader of the Labour Party, he said to me: "What do you think should be done with the party now?'

"I said: 'The short answer is to Sedgefieldise it."

John Burton: The Grit in the Oyster

"Perhaps I should have said 'burtonise it' but since John dislikes the cult of personality so intensely, I'll spare his blushes."

This, then, is the story of the man who put the burton into 'burtonise' and who helped put Tony Blair into No 10.

1: Friendship is constant

ONE of the small but most telling indicators of the value which Prime Minister Tony Blair places on his County Durham constituency is that, while other MPs talk about travelling "up to London" at the start of the Parliamentary week and "going down" at weekends, he almost always explains that, whenever time allows, he comes "up to Sedgefield" from Westminster and then goes "back down to London".

In talking this way, Blair is not devaluing his office as leader of the country; rather, he is reinforcing the fact that his Sedgefield constituency is where his Parliamentary career began.

Without Sedgefield there would have been, in all probability, no Westminster for him, and so no premiership. Without a tiny mediaeval village called Trimdon and the blind faith of a handful of locals, there would not even have been the Sedgefield, or any other, constituency.

Blair knows that. And he regularly mentions it in public because he knows there is still a debt to be repaid.

In the early hours of June 8, 2001, he mentioned it once more. From the stage in Trimdon Labour Club, with the election results coming in all the time and confirming an historic second term for Labour with an historic second landslide, he said: "You here have been the absolute rock on which I have built everything I have achieved. I have learned so much from you. You are the people who taught me the politics I now represent, and for that I thank you from the bottom of my heart."

When in Trimdon making a set piece speech, Blair usually speaks over the heads of the 100 or so local party members seated on the dancefloor. Instead he addresses the nation – and beyond – via the media and their cameras crammed on the balcony.

But this time, he forgot about the live national television audience watching the unfolding landslide, and he spoke specifically to those rocks in the room, and to one rock in particular – his agent John Burton.

While carrying out his national and international duties, Blair has to rely on others, primarily Burton, to run the constituency and to keep him closely informed about everything that goes on there.

Blair trusts Burton implicitly to speak with his authority on all constituency and related matters. The telephone in the Prime Minister's constituency office where Burton works is rarely silent. Nor is the one in the Burton household. Burton is always on call.

John Burton: The Grit in the Oyster

The constituency office in Blair's home is a mile or so from Trimdon Labour Club. The Burton household is just a couple of hundred yards from the club, and it was in the Burton home in Trimdon Village, that Blair and Burton first met in 1983.

Blair recalls: "It was a very curious thing; it was like meeting a soul mate. He struck me as a very interesting person. I'd been kicking around all sorts of constituency parties trying to get nominations and people were just ordinary people. Suddenly I came across someone who was unique."

Ever since that first meeting, the pair have been firm friends. A special bond has grown between them. Each values highly the attributes, knowledge, strengths, skills, expertise and opinions of the other.

As Blair says: "John has an extraordinarily instinctive ability as to where the public is on any issue, which makes him very valuable as a source of judgement. I often check a judgement against his. Often on major political issues I will pick up the phone and say, even in the middle of a crisis or difficulty, 'what's your sense of this?'.

"I have very rarely, if ever, known him to be wrong about a big political issue but he also has this ability to understand where other people are coming from. John is a highly intelligent man. It's something that people don't quite understand. They see the shrewdness, but he is highly intelligent.

"My view of John is, and always has been, that had he taken different turnings earlier in his life, and had maybe just a little more basic ambition, he would have gone very, very far indeed. I'm the beneficiary of the fact that he didn't."

Peter Mandelson also has the highest regard not only for John Burton the man and the politician but also for the way in which he fulfils his role as Tony Blair's agent.

"There is a selflessness about John, not only because he's a very dedicated, a very loyal member of the Labour Party and he would always think in terms of the best interests of the Labour Party rather than his own, but also at an individual level," says Mandelson, whose Hartlepool constituency neighbours Blair's Sedgefield. "He's not somebody to push himself forward; he doesn't particularly like to be in the limelight; he doesn't draw attention to himself and that, of course, has been very important because as the agent to the Prime Minister, the Prime Minister relies completely on his discretion, his loyalty, again his selflessness. These have been John's hallmarks, the reason why Tony, throughout, has looked to him for his wisdom and judgement.

"He's also relied upon him to represent him; the agent is somebody who speaks all the time with the authority of the Member of Parliament, in this case the Prime Minister.

"You can imagine the difficulty that would arise if his agent, John, spoke in a way that was out of step with Tony's views or was pushing his own views forward at the expense of Tony's. It would be impossible."

Mandelson also knows that there is more to Burton than just loyalty to his boss. He says: "What struck me about John immediately were not only his wisdom and his judgement about people and situations but his humour, his sense of fun, his sense of mischief but without any malign content to it whatsoever. That sunny face, the smile, bright eyes that would light up when they were telling a story or just when they were seeing the funny side of something; he's a brilliant raconteur who sees the fun, the humour in different situations and that makes him tremendous company."

Peter Mandelson was also one of the first to understand why Burton and Blair make such a dynamic team.

"They are kindred spirits," he says. "They have similar personalities, similar characters. They are both quite self-effacing. There's not a hint of arrogance or hauteur about either of them which is why, of course, Tony slipped and merged so well and so easily into the constituency and became such a natural in Trimdon and at the Labour Club. Tony can go back there and just switch off. Whatever he's been doing during the week, whoever he's been with, wherever he's been in the world, he can just sit down in the Labour Club surrounded by John and the others."

Mandelson believes that another of Burton's strengths, from which he feels the younger Blair learned a lot, is the way he conducts constituency business.

"John of course is very commanding," says the Hartlepool MP. "Let's not forget that this essentially saintlike character rules the place with a rod of iron. I have so many times over the years heard Tony describing John's behaviour at a constituency party meeting or how John shut somebody up or stopped this person in their tracks, how he dealt with this or resolved that.

"John is a very nice person; he's a very kind person but he's also a very hard and decisive person in his management of the local constituency party. Tony would sometimes come from a constituency meeting, which they always hold on a Saturday morning and which are always well-attended, sort of open-eyed, goggle-eyed almost, at the way in which John has defused a situation or dealt with somebody or stopped some issue in its tracks."

Like Mandelson, Burton also played a crucial role in the modernising of the Labour Party in the late 1980s and early 1990s, preparing it for power once more in 1997. In fact, Burton and others in Trimdon had been doing so for a number of years before the 1983 General Election.

However, it was the catalytic meeting of the minds of Blair and Burton, admittedly with other inputs too, which clearly identified and catalogued the old party's problems and then formulated and shaped what would be its radical renaissance as "New Labour".

Blair is unstinting in his praise for Burton's enormous contribution to the process. He says: "There is no doubt at all that he was one of the principal architects of New Labour. He formed my own thinking to a significant degree. I would say in my own personal development, he was one of the four or five most influential people on me."

Blair continues: "In 1983, the Labour Party just divided into two groups: those who thought that the thing was completely hopeless because the party had gone mad – and those who were mad. To be fair, there was a third category of people who just didn't understand what was going on."

At that time, Blair was struggling to understand what was going on in London, and it came as something of a surprise to discover that away from the metropolis the same struggle was taking place in rural Sedgefield.

He recalls: "There were a few of us down in London who were trying to work out the fact that it wasn't that the Labour Party had to get back to where it had been but that it had to modernise to where it had to be in the future. Therefore, the party shouldn't be presented with a choice between a very unreconstructed old Right-Wing, which was made up of basically very decent and good people who were a bit old-fashioned in their own way, and a sort of revolutionary Left that was, it was perfectly obvious, going to commit electoral suicide if it got charge of the Labour Party.

"When I first talked to John, I could see that he was asking the same types of questions about the Labour Party. He understood what the problem of the Left was and he also understood why the Left was wrong in what it was trying to do. He knew why it was in that position; such perception is a very rare thing.

"Here is the political importance of John; what we were trying to create was something in the Labour Party that left behind both the old Right and the old Left.

"The old Right was very much based on the trade unions sorting the Labour Party out and then letting the activists do whatever they wanted. In Hugh Gaitskell's time that was fine but in the modern world it doesn't work.

"The old Left was full of idealism but had got itself mixed up with a whole lot of university/Marxist nonsense and ended up with an analysis of the economy that was just totally unrealistic.

"My position was so modern in the sense that I didn't really have a constituency in either of those two camps. I thought that what the Labour Party should do was strip away everything other than its values and rebuild from there.

Those values are of community, social justice, belief in society as important to advancing the individual – very basic concepts, solidarity. Then we had to say to ourselves: 'Actually, those values need to be totally retranslated for the world today in economic policy, social policy and in the Labour Party itself'."

Blair continues: "This, in a sense, was what Neil Kinnock was trying to do but we didn't have much of a constituency within the party then, and I was very, very much in the modernist wing. Now here's the importance of my own Sedgefield constituency to this: I was arguing for a Labour Party which was mass membership, which involved the party members, one member/one vote, all that type of stuff. The old Right, which wanted to fix it through the trade union movement, wasn't exactly wild about that agenda really. The Left didn't like it because it wanted a sort of activist-based culture and, of course, we were hugely debilitated by the fact that in the early 1980s the SDP was taking away a whole generation of bright, young intellectuals, professional people and all the rest of it.

"The importance of Sedgefield to me was that we built here what the model of the New Labour Party, as we conceived it, should be: broad, open, sensible, serious, mass-membership. Therefore my constituency party was my protection all the way through the late 1980s and early 1990s, until just before I became leader, when people said of me: 'Oh, he's just the SDP'. It was a way of undermining people like myself and the Labour Party, and my defence was to say: 'Look, we're creating something here that isn't about leaving the Labour Party behind; it's actually about renewing the Labour Party'.

"And people like John would go out, give interviews, as would Paul (Trippett), Phil (Wilson) and Peter (Brookes), and people would say: 'Hang on; these people seem sensible. They've obviously got their roots in the local community. You can't accuse them of being careerists; you can't say that they're London SDP and all the rest of it'. They enhanced the whole credibility of what I was trying to do.

"So the constituency party is not just my relationship with John. What we created in Sedgefield was an exemplar of what the Labour Party should be and was a huge bulwark defending me against the charges of careerism and opportunism or whatever within the Labour Party."

Peter Mandelson agrees that Sedgefield and Burton helped shape Blair's view of the party. "Tony's thinking about modernisation predated his coming to Sedgefield," says Mandelson. "His thinking was rooted in the early 1980s and his experience of the Labour Party in London; but without any shadow of a doubt his analysis of the Labour Party, his understanding of it, deepened radically after he came to Sedgefield and spent hours, and I mean hundreds of hours, talking to John. He talked to others, of course, but John was the main kindred and guiding spirit in Tony's thinking because what John gave him was a vindication and reaffirmation of what he thought, and John also brought to it dimensions rooted in a very long-standing Labour Party community which Tony didn't have from his membership of the party in London. That's very important."

Mandelson also believes that Burton was vital not just as Blair's lightning conductor to protect him against accusations of careerism, but as the man who opened the door to Labour's heartlands.

Mandelson says: "Our commitment to modernisation sprang from a number of things, chiefly a desire to see the Labour Party stop losing. That meant serious questioning as to why the Labour Party was not winning support. People often asked: 'What's that got to do with the North? The Labour Party wins in the North. Why do we need modernisation?'.

"There are two responses to that which John Burton articulated as well as anyone else. First of all, if you want to win a General Election in this country it's no good simply banking up support in the North. Unless you win the Midlands, the South and London, you are a fringe party and useless to everyone. Also what John saw much more than the rest of us, because the North had always been his patch, was that not only did people in the North tire of the Labour Party not winning other parts of the country and therefore not doing them any good because they were in opposition but also people in the North saw in the Labour Party an organisation that was in many respects becoming moribund, taking previous successes for granted, not renewing itself, not challenging itself, not making itself work harder, not thinking about new and different ways in which it could recruit members, and how it could involve individuals in its political work. Those points were as relevant and important in the North as anywhere else.

"People thought that just because the Labour Party had been returned in one election after another in the North it didn't need to question any more deeply what it did, how it did it, how it represented people, how it got more people into the party, how it revitalised itself, how it renewed itself. John was always a thinker about that!"

Reinforcing Blair's words, Mandelson is keen to stress Burton's role in the modernising process. He says: "John was one of the principal architects of New Labour. What John gave to Tony was a hinterland, a knowledge in depth, a feel, an experience, a reach into the Labour Party, its history, its soul, its human make-up. Via John and that marvellous schoolmasterly way that John has of educating people, Tony was able to acquire through his own instinctive grasp and understanding of situations a knowledge of what made people tick."

Mo Mowlam, until 2001 the MP for nearby Redcar, also stresses Burton's role in the modernisation of the Labour Party. "John was crucial in the organisation of New Labour. Without him, Tony would not have got the Sedgefield seat and history would have been very different," she says.

"Nothing's ever too much trouble for John; he's always ready to help. He was also vital to the early years of Tony's career, to his development and his thinking; under John's tutelage, Tony grew as a person. Tony respects him very much and envies who he is, his ease of living."

Part of Burton's "ease of living" comes from his intuitive ability to understand those around him. "What John understands is people and what they need to equip themselves to make a success of their lives," says Mandelson. "That is not simply formal educational qualifications, important as those are, but the informal education, the development of character, of potential, the need to stretch people, to challenge them, to make them both confident about themselves and ambitious about what they can achieve.

"Now if you take that quality together with his pioneering spirit, John is without prejudice to new ideas, to new ways of doing things. John has a great sense of history, very powerful roots but he's an innovator. That's what was so important for New Labour.

"Why did Sedgefield Constituency Labour Party turn itself into the largest and one of the most active mass-membership parties in the country? It was because of John's embrace of new ideas, his leadership qualities, his ability to make sense of things for people who might otherwise be unsure about them and be fearful of change.

"John is reassuring; he interprets, he guides, he draws people along and makes them feel confident and happy about change and that is a rare quality in somebody. It's why his relationship to New Labour is so important. He gave it depth, he gave it legitimacy, he gave it a human feel, a roundedness that perhaps others of us couldn't give, either because we were steeped in theoretical policy or the practice of communications or whatever.

"John gave it humanity and that is very important. That's what he brings to whatever he touches, to whatever he comes into contact with, the people, the organisations, whatever. He humanises situations, he humanises problems and dilemmas.

"What John brings to any situation, what he's given to Tony, what he's given to the Labour Party, is an ability to humanise, to impart wisdom and to do so with wit. Now that is an important and unique blend of skills. Some people can have one or two of those things, not usually all of them; John has and that's what makes him such a powerful personality. I say powerful and immediately think:

John Burton: The Grit in the Oyster

'How can somebody who is so decent and so modest be so powerful?'. But he is, through sheer dint of his personality and his ability to guide people, to win their trust and their affection and to persuade them to his point of view.

"Now that's power!"

2: The eye of childhood

THE Parliamentary constituency of Sedgefield nestles between the rivers Wear and Tees in the North-East of England. It is a land of contrasts where those who want to find a stereotyped Andy Capp figure among the allotments and pigeon lofts will do so. But also, rising from the reclaimed pitheaps and landscaped ironworks there is to be found new light industry and comfortable new homes.

There are former colliery villages, terraced houses and working men's clubs where the most frequent request at the bar is for 'a pint please, pet'. Barmaids do not hear this 'pet' as a sexist term; it is as much a part of the local language and lore as are 'hinney' and 'marrer', long-established and accepted 'pitmatic' terms of endearment and friendship which linger, almost lovingly, from a former time.

There are also whippets, greyhounds, pigeon lofts (known locally as 'crees'), allotments (once the miners' temporary escape from the blackness of the pit), and characters who wear flat caps, perhaps with a cigarette dangling from their lips, and speak a Durham dialect – not a 'Geordie' accent, for in some things they are still tribal: Sunderland, not Newcastle, is very much the football club of the constituency.

This is the element on which unknowing or naïve outsiders, who have come in search of Andy Capp, usually focus, unable to look past their nose ends. The nose end, however, is a notoriously dangerous place to stop.

Four-bedroomed detached houses with double garages are now also a common sight and holidays overseas are as familiar a part of life as the traditional fortnight in a boarding house at Whitley Bay used to be.

The Sedgefield constituency is proud not only of its past; it can also boast about its revival and rebirth.

Once upon a time, and not so very long ago, this was the land of Category D villages, communities which, it had been decided, were too run-down to be saved and would cost too much to build again. No future money was to be wasted developing them.

They were consigned to a long and lingering death by Durham County council in a 1951 plan that was sanctioned by the Government in 1954. To use a medical analogy, the Council would not actually hasten their demise but it would withhold any further treatment.

Those who lived in these villages, salt-of-the-earth people whose history and heritage were enshrined in frequently dilapidated buildings, pit-heaps and obscure folklore, were not, however, going to allow their past, and their future, to be demolished at a stroke without a fight.

One of the Category D villages, Trimdon Grange, had been, after all, the birthplace of one of the North's greatest political leaders, Peter Lee. He had come from mining stock, been a miner himself and had risen to become, in 1919, the first chairman of Durham County Council – the first such body in the country ever to be controlled by Labour. He, the great Peter Lee, it was argued, would never have sanctioned what the people regarded as nothing less than the murder of their communities.

And these were places which had been established by their forebears, by men, women and children who had lived through appalling hardship, abject poverty, unimaginable disaster and untold anguish to stake their claim to a future which was, in their own time, little more than an impossible dream.

They triumphed. In the early 1960s, the Category D battle was won. The villages were spared, grudgingly some still believe, and allowed to live to fight for a future. Since then, they have experienced varying degrees of investment and regeneration and some, like Peter Lee's Trimdon Grange, have been completely transformed.

Those looking no further than the end of their nose will not see that there is far more to the Sedgefield constituency than former colliery villages fighting for survival in the post-mining economy. There are as many settlements which have existed since Saxon times, attractive places which have changed little in the past two or three centuries. Even their mediaeval layouts are still as easily spotted as the ancient rig and furrow ploughmarks in the surrounding fields.

At the other end of the scale is the 'new town' of Newton Aycliffe, created just after the last war.

This is a green and pleasant, gently-rolling rural landscape, criss-crossed by winding country roads with neat hedges and intersected by the busy dual carriageways of the A1M and the A19. To the north lie the treasures of the City of Durham whose Norman cathedral and castle are now a World Heritage site, plus Peterlee, a new town named after Trimdon Grange's famous son.

To the south are Darlington, birthplace of the railways, and Croft-on-Tees, boyhood home of Charles Lutwidge Dodgson, a mathematics genius better remembered by the world as the writer Lewis Carroll. Over to the west lie two of British tourism's best-kept secrets, the beautiful Weardale and Teesdale, down whose tracks in former times Scottish raiders gained illicit access to the rich pickings of this fertile region. Further to the east is the grey, unforgiving North Sea with the headland of Hartlepool, one of the first cradles of Christianity in England – and, incidentally, the birthplace of Andy Capp.

Commerce and light industry also flourish here in Sedgefield, an entirely different source of employment for those who once worked in coal mines and shipyards. Coal used to be king in this place but few, in retrospect, grieve for his passing. The new industry is clean and increasingly green. More of it will always be welcome, hence the on-going trade missions and quiet conversations to entice global companies to a place where there is a ready supply of skilled and adaptable labour, as the Japanese motor giant Nissan discovered in nearby Sunderland.

This Sedgefield, then, is where John Burton lives, the land he is proud to call home, whose people he holds in such high regard.

He was born at 14, West Lane in Trimdon Village, one of the area's ancient settlements, and has lived there almost all of his life.

He was born on September 8, 1940; the Battle of Britain was being fought out in Britain's skies and the country's future hung in the balance. It was, in fact, the day after the Luftwaffe changed its tactics and instead of attempting to destroy fighter airfields began mounting massed bomber raids on London in retaliation for a Royal Air Force attack on the Berlin area.

John's father, Donald, was serving on battleships and in the Education Corps as a lieutenant in the Royal Navy, the branch of the armed forces for which he had volunteered. His mother, Dorothy, had previously suffered seven miscarriages and was understandably overjoyed at the birth of this healthy baby boy. He was ultimately to follow his father into the teaching profession, into local politics (Donald Burton served on Sedgefield Rural District Council) and into the post of churchwarden at the local church on the green, the 12th Century St Mary Magdalene.

The boy attended church regularly, as did all of his young friends. Membership of the choir and Sunday school were indelible elements of his formative years. The church and singing are still important in his life today. His childhood was not much affected by the war although he still has memories of travelling by train to see his father, when his ship was in port, to the likes of Saltash, on the south coast near Plymouth, to Rosyth, across the Firth of Forth from Edinburgh, and even way up to Gare Loch, north-west of Glasgow. These were epic expeditions, positive odysseys for a youngster to make, clutching his brown paper bag of sandwiches tightly as he journeyed to what seemed to be the ends of the earth. Jam sandwiches, he recalls, did not travel well, nor did those containing that staple wartime filling, condensed milk. But, he says, they still tasted really good when you were hungry.

At that time, they could take the train from Trimdon Colliery or even from Hurworth Burn, a station about three miles to the east of Trimdon Village. Or they could catch a bus into Durham City and then climb the steep bank to the railway station with its magnificent view of the cathedral and castle.

Trimdon Village was even quieter then than it is today. Children could play almost anywhere, on the roads or in the fields, and play they did. Soccer and cricket were the favoured games and the teams were picked without any thought for political correctness: sometimes it was "Phil Fellows and John Burton pick" because they were the two best sportsmen; other times it was "top end versus bottom end", and sometimes it was "Protestants v Catholics".

Different fields served different purposes according to their special attributes, their use, or otherwise, dictated by the prevailing moods of their owners.

Edgar's Field, the property of a farmer called Edgar Tinkler, near the footpath on the way down to Trimdon Grange, had a flat part and so cricket was played there. On a fine day, Edgar used to sit on the fence at the top and watch as the 20 or more youngsters showed off their juvenile skills. For two hours, or longer, he was content to leave them alone but then he would suddenly decide that he had enjoyed enough entertainment. Climbing down from his perch, he would shout at the boys, telling them in no uncertain terms to get off his land, which they duly did, remembering to grab the makeshift stumps as they fled. A few hours later, usually after having had a meal, they would return to the same field and again Edgar would repeat the same ritual.

Tot's Field, owned by Tot Redfern, farmer and local milkman, was better suited to football and it was further away from his farmhouse than Edgar's Field was from Edgar's. Most of the time, he left well alone but one day, when the boys had tired of football and turned to cricket, Tot descended on the game and ended it by walking off with the stumps. As John says today: "That wasn't really cricket, was it?" He was to confiscate the stumps several more times after that but always returned them eventually.

One day the itinerant sportsmen found a safer home where they could play undisturbed. John's father had a word with Alec Kirkpatrick who consented to games being played on one or other of the fields at his farm, Catley Hill, a mile or so outside the village but, since most of the youngsters had bikes, this was no problem. They even played on stubble after the harvest had been gathered in but, as long as it was a field of some sort, the condition mattered little. They were magical, rose-coloured spectacle days when play was the essence of the boys' lives.

As John grew older and played with an even greater passion, Donald Burton would occasionally borrow cricket bats, pads and real stumps from the school where he taught so that the lads could be properly kitted out.

The Burtons' house in West Lane had a garden to the rear. Beyond a small section of lawn lay a vegetable garden which Donald loved to plant and look after. During the war years, neighbours helped to keep it as it should be. Donald stretched a taut piece of string between two sticks as a guide to sowing seeds in straight, neat rows and raised good, if not prize-winning, crops.

As John grew older, he liked to help his father with the weeding. Both of them shied away from working on the strawberry patch but when it looked completely out of control and overgrown they pulled together to restore it to some semblance of normality. They hated the job except when the strawberries were ripe because then they could pick them illicitly, both pretending not to have seen the other at this nefarious activity. When Mrs Burton enquired why the crop seemed so poor, they blamed the slugs and snails.

At the end of the garden, just out into the neighbouring field, stood an Anderson air-raid shelter which was shared by several families at the top end of the street. It remained there long after hostilities had ceased. One of John's earliest memories is of sitting on a bench in the shelter with his mother and the next-door neighbours, Mr and Mrs Partridge. He sensed that, because they were all down there, something must be wrong but he was unsure what it was. No bombs fell on Trimdon Village but an enemy aeroplane did come down in Tot's Quarry, the property of that same Tot Redfern who would later disrupt the boys' cricket matches. Perhaps he had tried to chase the German pilot off his land too, John muses.

Sometimes Donald would come home on leave, usually for three days. Dorothy and John were delighted to see him but on one occasion he was still at home after almost a week. When Dorothy asked if he would not get into trouble for being away too long from his ship he replied that if he missed it at one port he would catch it at the next – and he did.

When Donald was eventually demobbed, life changed forever for John. Being an only child, the boy had been used to sitting up late, often until eleven o'clock at night or even later, keeping his mother company. But his father sent him to bed at six o'clock. When Mrs Burton went upstairs to tuck him in, John's first question was: "When's he going back to sea?" He never did! The newly-imposed curfew was there to stay but, even now, John finds that there is no point in retiring much before midnight; he simply cannot fall asleep.

Rationing, of both food and clothes, was something about which the young Burton and his mother sometimes talked. It was to be the early 1950s before it ceased to be a problem. John remembers that almost every little girl in the village had a winter 'pixie' hat, hand-knitted, and that many of the lads wore short trousers which were really long trousers, cast-offs from older relatives, cut short to fit. He felt somehow different because, not having any brothers or sisters, he never had any such 'hand-me-downs'.

Whale meat was one of the foods on the Burton family's wartime diet. Many have argued with John that such a thing never existed but he maintains that it was a fairly regular culinary item, even if not terribly pleasant to the palate. Nevertheless, that wonderful cook Marguerite Patten tried very hard in her wartime wireless broadcasts to persuade the British that it could be both nourishing and tasty. She failed to convince the Burton household.

One of the greatest mysteries of the food rationing era was the banana. John had never seen one but a lesson at school had been about this fruit and the places where it was grown. "The islands, in the West Indies, were so far away that they might as well have been on the moon," he recalls. Although he does not remember doing so, John must have plagued his mother about the banana and its taste. One day he came home from school and enjoyed one of his mother's wonderful stews, which she always made with soft dumplings. Grandma was als there. His plate so clean that it did not need washing, John asked what was for pudding. Mother produced a bowl filled with a yellowy-brown substance. "What is it?" he asked. On being told that it was mashed banana, he tasted a spoonful. It was not at all what he had expected but, since bananas were so rare, he ate the lot and claimed to have enjoyed it. In truth, he did not. Not at all.

A few years later when he was at Grandma's house for tea, she asked him if he would like a banana. It was only after he had politely refused and explained why that she told him that the 'banana' he had previously tasted had really been boiled parsnip mashed up with butter, sugar and a little banana essence and topped with mock cream. He is wary of bananas even now. Nor has he ever tasted tomato sauce or similar brown ones. His mother always had Bovril on the side of her plate of fish, or egg, and chips and he does the same to this day.

To use ration books, families had to register with specific shops. The Burtons went to Wilkinson's at the bottom of the street to buy such wartime staples as Spam. John quite liked that and still does. Their butcher was Mr Thompson who traded in the main street in what is now a house where his grandsons live. On a good day, at the right time, even a few sausages could be bought there but 'a pound of scrag end' was the more usual offering.

Mrs Burton was an exceptionally good cook who prepared tasty, wholesome food and could make a little go a long way. Yorkshire puddings were a speciality of hers, made the 'proper' way in a large, deep oven tray and, like so many other Northern matriarchs, she always promised on a Sunday that those who ate the most Yorkshire pudding would get the most meat. Needless to say, those who ate the most Yorkshire pudding had little room left for very much meat!

Today, in retrospect, John still continues to be amazed that so many families managed to have breakfast, dinner (as lunch is called in the North-East), tea then supper, four good meals a day even when rationing was at its worst. Supper was always a cooked 'something'.

One of the best dinners of the week was always served on Mondays. This was 'fry-up', the leftovers from Sunday lunch when, quite deliberately, too many vegetables were cooked so that they could be used in this Monday treat. The Yorkshire pudding that remained, and there always was some even if the meat had gone, was added to the frying pan last and then the entire meal was served with rich onion gravy. It is still a Northern delicacy today. Even such a staple as stew, or 'a few broth', as older people used to call it, was, and is still, better the day after it is made.

Another 'leftover' which was popular in the Burton house was what his father called 'fairy soup'; to a youngster, the name suggested a magic ingredient but, in truth, it was simply yesterday's gravy with a few spare vegetables added.

A classic feature of village life was the delivery man, and there were several of them. At first, they would come with a horse and cart but most graduated to vans. One was Alf, the 'store chemist'. The 'store' was the Northern name for the Co-op, in Trimdon's case the Station Town, Seaham and Horden Co-operative Wholesale Society which had a branch at the crossroads at the top of the main street. The manager was Mr Hardy. The fruiterer, Freddie Lee, also called, as did Santi, the ice cream man from Fishburn. Mrs Burton bought gallon tins of olive oil from him at a time when very few people cooked with it, preferring fat or lard instead.

The Burton home was always full of people. Many were John's friends: Jim, Colin and George Seymour, Paul Robinson, Phil Dodds, Eric Cullen and Phil Fellows. They all lived in each other's houses, but Burton's was where you could play subbuteo or cards and get your supper before going home. John feels it was because his parents realised he was an only child and so needed the company of others – a need that has stayed with him all his life.

Other callers came to see Donald on church or council business. The local vicar, Captain Baker, was a regular visitor. He was a retired naval officer and having been a captain while Donald had been a mere lieutenant he always referred to him simply as "Burton". One day when he called unexpectedly, the family was just about to go out. "Going somewhere nice, are you?" he enquired. Donald replied that they were off to the cinema in Hartlepool to see the new film Scott Of The Antarctic. "Ah yes," said the vicar, "Scott. Nice young fellow. Served under me once. Yes, a good sort."

It was quite a revelation for the whole family to realise that they were going to see a film about a national hero who had once served on the same ship as their local vicar. To John, in retrospect, this was living history. He had heard about Scott at school but Captain Baker had really known him, talked to him, worked with the man.

The Burtons had a grey tabby tomcat, a fierce creature, called Pongo and all the local dogs, no matter how big, were absolutely terrified of him. He would take on any of them with just one exception. The vicar had a blind dog and if it came into the room before Pongo saw it, the cat would leap onto the sideboard, jump over Captain Baker's head and flee out of the back door. He could not bear to be in the same room as that dog and would not come back into the house for several hours after its departure.

The local window cleaner called on the same day every week and one day he brought with him his dog, a huge, aggressive beast as John recalls. "Down Jippo," he kept telling it. "Get down."

"Why do you keep saying that?" Donald asked as the big dog growled on. "Well," replied the tradesman, "your cat's lying under that laburnum tree there and, if I let it, my dog would kill him."

Donald had a wry sense of humour so he encouraged the window cleaner to instruct his dog to attack Pongo. At last, the visitor gave the command. "Get him," he cried and the dog hurtled across the little lawn towards the cat.

Within seconds, after the briefest but most vicious of fights, Pongo was resting, like Alice's Cheshire cat, on a branch of the tree while the dog fled, whimpering, from the garden. It was three full days before the dog returned to its own home. Presumably, it had been licking its wounds – and there had been several – but it never again entered the Burton property.

Some years later, Pongo went off on his travels, as was his way, usually returning after two or three days. This time he never returned. Perhaps he had at last met his match on one of the local farms. He had been with John for most of his childhood and was sadly missed.

One day the local builder, Mark Walker, called in at the house. His wife was treasurer to the church council. His visits were times when Donald would take out the whisky bottle. After they had emptied a few glasses, Mark explained the reason he had stopped by. He had been building a bungalow on one of the last pieces of ground to be vacant in the village and when digging out the foundations he had uncovered a perfectly preserved Roman mosaic pavement. In this part of Britain, such a mosaic indicated beyond any doubt that a Roman or Romano-British villa had once stood on that site and, in the very early 1950s, it would have been one of the most northerly then known. The only other one nearby had been a few miles further north at Old Durham but that has long since fallen victim to quarrying. Even very recently, however, Roman coins have turned up in Trimdon Village which occupies one of the highest pieces of ground on the coastal plain and would have been a superb strategic site for the Romans and for those who came after them, with excellent views for miles around. North of York, such luxury homesteads seem to have been extremely rare. Sadly, the builder had not even photographed it; he simply covered it with soil because, had he made the find public, his building work would have been halted while an archaeological rescue excavation was carried out and he could not have afforded such a delay.

The wireless, which stood beside the fireplace in the dining room, was one of the Burtons' most popular forms of entertainment. It was one of those wooden-cased models with a round top and brown cloth covering the loudspeaker. Long before the days of frequency-modulation and high-fidelity, there was often some interference, "atmospherics" as it was usually termed. John loved comedy shows, especially ITMA (It's That Man Again) and was also very fond of the boxing. The whole family would gather round the set to hear the blow-by-blow commentaries. He wonders how on earth he managed to follow what was happening since he had never actually seen a real boxing match either live or even on the newsreel at the cinema.

Later, The Goon Show took his fancy and he became a great fan. The Dreaded Batter Pudding Hurler of Bexhill-on-Sea and Tales of Men's Shirts – A Story of Down Under were among his favourite episodes with Spike Milligan, Harry Secombe, Peter Sellers and the rest unravelling the unlikely and, to the uninitiated, unfathomable plots. Indeed, Burton's oft-remarked upon sense of humour today could owe its origin, he suggests, to those programmes.

John's mother had taught him to read before he went to Trimdon Village school at the age of five and he loved reading. There had always been books around the house; they were on every shelf – King Solomon's Mines, The Modern Teacher, A Traveller Abroad and dozens more. His mother had often scolded his dad for leaving them, open and face down, on any and every flat surface.

It was his father who had introduced John to the works of his favourite childhood author, Captain WE Johns and the character Biggles. He can still remember the first thrill of reading about the adventures of this boys' hero, Captain James Bigglesworth, Royal Flying Corps (RFC). Johns had himself been a pilot in the RFC and, later, in the Royal Air Force and he wrote from experience. Biggles, Algy, Ginger and Bertie became a part of Burton's young life, and friends who were not reading the same literature were soon excluded from some conversations.

WE Johns wrote more than 70 Biggles books and John has read every one and has possessed in his time, but not today, several first editions. "Where did I leave them?" he wonders. He also enjoyed the books about those other WE Johns' characters, Gimlet, a commando, and Worrals, a member of the Women's Auxiliary Air Force.

"I didn't dare tell my mates that I read books about her," he is prepared to admit today. "They'd never have spoken to me again. But, there again, that was then!"

As a boy, John used to suffer from bronchitis every year without fail and was often confined to bed for up to a month at a time, the persistent coughing weakening him considerably. Mr Kirkpatrick, the farmer at Catley Hill who allowed his fields to be played on, told his parents not to worry because, he assured them, he would grow out of it. To pass the long hours, John would knit squares for Dr Barnado's. He remembers the simple instructions from his mother: "In, over, through then off." The squares were later stitched together to make blankets.

Another pastime was based on the old cardboard milk bottle tops. A hole would be made in the middle of one and then wool was wrapped through it. When no more wool could be forced through, the edges were cut and the resulting pom-pom was given to the local church – although John never knew to what use they were put.

The war did touch John's life in one way which he has never forgotten. His Aunt Connie, his father's sister, had married an Italian called Tony Massarella who had an ice cream shop at Herrington Burn, near Sunderland. He had never applied to become a British citizen and so when war broke out he was interned as an alien on the Isle of Man, where he was not looked after very well. Simply because she was his wife, Connie was perceived to be a threat to national security and had to live a specified distance away from the coast, presumably so that she could not contact enemy warships or submarines. As a result, she moved in with the Burtons in Trimdon Village since her own home was too close to the sea. At first, she had to report once a week to the police at Houghton-le-Spring but, after a lot of negotiating, Donald managed to have this ruling changed so that she could report instead to the local police station.

When the war was over, John's parents took him on holiday for a month every summer to the town of Dollar in south-east Scotland. This was not an extravagance since Donald was actually house-sitting for a former naval colleague, Ivor Lawrence, who went, with his wife Joy, to visit relatives in Swanage. Donald never possessed a car, although he could drive, so this was another adventure by train.

John loved being in this old Scottish town and made friends with the local lads. One day he suggested that they should have a game of cricket but not only did they not have a bat and ball, they did not even know the rules. Settling instead for a climb up to what were then the ruins of the old castle, John resolved to bring his own cricketing paraphernalia the following year, which he duly did and introduced his Gaelic friends to the subtleties of the game. His father was none too happy about having bat, ball, stumps and bails as part of the holiday luggage and had drawn the line at taking two sets of pads as well, but when he saw the first game in progress, he could not resist joining in.

It was in Dollar that John first encountered a bee-keeper. With his thick, white suit, huge gloves and netted headgear, he was unlike anything the boy had seen before. Why should anyone in their right mind want to 'invade' the home of thousands of bees, he wondered? Why was he puffing smoke at them? Surely that would make them even more irate.

From a safe distance, John sat on an old stone wall and watched the antics of the apiarist. When the man had finished, he removed his strange hat and went into a little wooden hut a few yards away from the beehives.

Emerging a few minutes later, he walked along the road towards where John was sitting. A few words were exchanged, essentially about the weather. The bee-keeper realised immediately that this was not a local youth. Was the lad from Newcastle, he asked? John explained that he was from County Durham. He never thought to explain precisely where that was.

As the days passed, he became increasingly fascinated by the bee-keeper. Sometimes he would just sit on the wall and watch what he did; on other occasions there would be a brief conversation. All the time he wondered why anyone would lay himself open to being seriously stung when he had no need to do so. One morning, dismal and wet, not at all the sort of day for cricket, John sat on his wall and watched the bee-keeper. Just as he was tiring of this pastime, the man shouted to him: "Hold on laddie; I've something for you."

The bee-keeper went into the hut to remove his special garb. A few minutes later he emerged with a greaseproof paper parcel in his hands.

"This is for you and your folks," he said. "Do you like honey?"

"Oh, yes. Thank you very much," John replied.

In truth, the boy had never even tasted the delicacy before but, when he returned to the cottage, his mother was delighted with the gift, a whole comb of honey, wax and all.

In Trimdon Village, the local policeman, the bobby, was a man called Hutchinson but he was always known as "Hutchy" and the local children held him in awe; he really was a man to be feared, or so they thought. He was certainly to be respected. He once stopped John for giving a friend a lift on his bike; two on a bike was not only illegal but also against the laws of nature as far as Hutchy was concerned. He even went round to the family home and gave the lads a severe dressing down in front of Mr and Mrs Burton.

Many years later, Hutchy was to come to John's rescue. Several of the lads from the grammar school had decided to cycle to the Isle of Skye. They had looked at the map and concluded that it would be a reasonable expedition.

"We must have been mad," says John, "or not as good at geography as we thought. We had to cycle like idiots to make the distances between the youth hostels where we were staying. We were absolutely exhausted every single evening but we did get to Skye and we did it within the time we had allowed ourselves. Mind you, we could barely walk when we got there and we never did it again!" There and back again was about 800 miles.

The day before they were due to set off on this mammoth undertaking, John had an accident with his bike and was concerned about the front wheel. He could not see exactly what was wrong but knew that it was not as it should have been. Hutchy was a man who could fix practically anything so John went to see him in his shed. Within minutes, the wizard had "done the business" with the dodgy spokes and sent the boy on his way to prepare for the Scottish adventure. The policeman must have had an incredibly long memory because as John rode away he shouted after him: "And remember young Burton – just one to a bike."

Even John's father had a run-in with Hutchy soon after the war broke out. Donald, a founder member of the Local Defence Volunteers, later the Home Guard, was walking home one night when, at the crossroads, he knocked his pipe out against a garden wall. The sparks flew everywhere in the breeze. Suddenly, a familiar voice boomed out of the darkness: "Hey, you. You can't do that. A German pilot could see that from miles away." It was Hutchy.

"Sorry constable," Donald called back. "I won't do it again." As he made his way home, Donald chuckled to himself; the Germans were more likely to hear Hutchy, he thought, than they were to see the outpourings of his pipe.

On another occasion, an exercise was planned during which the local Home Guard was to defend Trimdon Village vicarage against an attack by regular troops. An elaborate plan was devised by 'the amateurs'. An entire day was spent making sure that nothing could possibly go wrong. They awaited the expected onslaught. As night fell and nothing seemed to be happening, they decided that a strong cup of tea should be the order of the day. Just as it had been brewed, they gathered in the kitchen, at which precise moment the regulars burst in, took them all prisoner and the exercise was over almost before it had begun. As Donald was marched out, hands above his head, he turned to his officer and said: "I did tell you that they'd smell the tea!"

Donald's father, Jesse Burton, is remembered for having started the first bus company in Sunderland and for having been the landlord of the Board Inn at East Herrington. His mother and brother, another Jesse Burton, subsequently ran an off-licence in the coastal village of Seaham Harbour. John, with his wry sense of humour, is still amused by the fact that there are not one but two "Jesses" in his family tree.

It was at Seaham, in 1815, that the poet Lord Byron was married to Anne Milbanke and where, in 1828, the 3rd Marquess of Londonderry began to build his harbour, a new port, for shipping coal. It was also at Seaham that John was introduced to cricket by Uncle Jess. The two of them travelled all over the county to support the Seaham Harbour team which played in the Durham Senior League with a brilliant professional, Dickie Fuller, the first West Indian sportsman John had seen. It was also Uncle Jess who, with Donald Burton's blessing, gave John his first pipe when he was just nine years old. John took a few puffs and was then violently sick. The idea was that it would put him off smoking for the rest of his life but the ploy did not work. Uncle Jess had spent his wartime years mainly in North Africa and Sicily and those years had taken their toll; he died when he was just 35 but John still treasures fond memories of their times together.

John's maternal grandfather, Edward Tarr, who lived at the Stack Yard near Shiney Row, had been gamekeeper to Lord Lambton and was known far and wide both as an expert in his field and as the man who, as a matter of habit, took a pet fox on a lead into the local hostelry when he went for a drink. History does not record whether the fox was also fond of beer.

Donald Burton, born in Philadelphia, between Newbottle and Shiney Row in County Durham, was a gentle person who eventually became headteacher at Sedgefield Secondary, an all age school such as existed in those days. His main subjects at the College of the Venerable Bede where he had trained in Durham City had been French and woodwork and his first job, in 1933, required him to travel between different schools to teach the latter. He started in Hesleden and then cycled to Trimdon Village and Trimdon Colliery. Subsequently, he journeyed between Sedgefield and Trimdon Village where he eventually gained a full time job. There, he was always referred to as 'Daddy' Burton, such was his reputation as a kindly and caring man. John is pleased that people still talk about him and remember him so fondly.

"You'll never be as good as your dad," they say.

"Nobody ever could be," he is proud to admit, "and nobody could ever pay me a greater compliment. He really was a wonderful man in so many ways."

3: A scholar, and a ripe good one

IN SEPTEMBER 1946, John Burton started school, technically at the age of five although his sixth birthday was just a few days away. All of his friends were in the year above him and he was the oldest child in his year when his mother took him along for his first day at Trimdon Village Parochial School. He was rather embarrassed and would much rather have gone on his own but would not have upset his mother for all the world.

It was an 'all-age' school since most pupils started their education there, aged about five, and left when they were 14 or 15, depending, for the most part, on whether their parents needed them to work in the family business, on the farm or in some other employment. Some of these older children simply drifted away from school when their time was almost up rather than leaving on a specified date. Their parents might have received a visit from the 'school board man', more popularly known as the 'kiddie-catcher', but few were worried by this. Truancy cases rarely went to court and, if the parents needed the child's labour or income to make ends meet, it was a risk they were prepared to run.

The village always thought that it was a Church of England school but when many years later it closed, the locals, and the Education Committee, were more than a little surprised to discover that it had been set up as a charity school, with money given by John and Henry Airey, and had been wrongly administered for years. The redundant school was to have been redesignated as a parish hall but the deeds declared that the building had to be used for educational purposes so classes of one sort or another had to be, and were, organised until the old place was finally demolished.

John's early schooldays were fairly uneventful but it was noticed that he was a very intelligent lad who knew his tables and could use them, read well and could write a good composition, as essays were called at the time. As long as he could understand why he was required to learn something, then he was happy to do so. He could never understand why, having once mastered the essentials of long multiplication and long division, he was required to work out what seemed like thousands of such sums in the succeeding months and years and, in English lessons, why he had to write over and over again about how he had spent his summer or Christmas holiday.

Even at this early age, he was playing for the school football team and to him that was one of the saving graces of the education system into which he had to fit.

When he was 11, he was required to sit what used to be called 'the scholarship', later 'the eleven plus', to decide whether he was to be offered a place at a grammar school. Because of his age, John's friends had taken the tests the year previously and had already gone on to secondary education elsewhere. In fact, John had been in their class until they had moved on because he was academically so far ahead of his peers. This meant that in his last year at primary, he had to repeat everything he had done in the previous year. He felt cheated.

The scholarship examination was in two parts, one taken at his own school, the other at the nearest grammar school. John, top of the class, was not too worried about the outcome. When the day arrived for the first part, all of the candidates were advised by the supervising teacher to read the paper carefully before beginning to write. He did as instructed, and then he read it several times more. Ten minutes passed. Eventually, the teacher walked down to John's desk and suggested that it might be a good idea if he were to start to write. This was against all the rules as there was supposed to be total silence and no communication whatsoever between the examinations officer and the pupils. He began to work and finished with time to spare.

His lasting memory of that day is of watching one of his friends, a boy not gifted academically, staring at the exam paper, chewing his pen, scratching his head and squirming in his seat. They might as well have given him a Hebrew text to translate into English, he recalls; no child should ever have been made to suffer like that.

After the exam, John found him in the playground and asked him how he thought he had done.

"Well, it wasn't all that easy," he replied, "but I did manage to write a bit more than my name. I don't think I've passed though." He had not.

For the second stage of the tests, John had to travel to nearby Wingate to the AJ Dawson Grammar School, later known as Wellfield School. He found out many years afterwards from his headmaster that he had the highest score in that second part. His parents were even more delighted than he was that he had gained a coveted grammar school place even though they would now have to find the money for a blazer, a new satchel and the rest of the uniform, including full PE kit.

Donald Burton was a Labour councillor and, in some ways against his better judgement and principles, he sent his son to Barnard Castle to try for a scholarship place at the famous boys' public school there, the County School as it was then popularly known. Some 200 took the entrance exam and John was horrified to be faced with the task of correctly placing colons and semi-colons into a piece of prose. He had never encountered such things before. They had never even existed at Trimdon Village School. This, to him, was punctuation gone mad.

He was placed seventh out of the 200 candidates and was offered entrance to the school but not on the hoped-for scholarship; those were awarded only to the top four or five and he had just missed out. The not inconsiderable fees would have had to be paid by his parents and might have been an unbearable strain on their budget but money was never discussed. The boy was actually happier to go to Wellfield, as everyone called the school even then, because most of his friends were there. One of his abiding memories is of the first day he put on the Wellfield blazer, hoisted his satchel over his shoulder and set off to catch the school bus which would take him the few miles down the road to Wingate.

The school was formally named after Sir Arthur James Dawson, a former chairman of Durham County Education Committee who had been born in 1859 and knighted in 1931. It had been opened in 1930 by the great Peter Lee. Coincidentally, its first chairman of governors had been Alderman George Robson who, in 1882, had been the youngest survivor of the dreadful Trimdon Grange explosion. Both Lee and Robson died in 1935 while Sir Arthur lived on until 1943.

John Burton remembers that one of the lads at the school noticed that a number of schools in the area were named after chairmen of the Education Committee. Take as an example the Alderman Wraith Grammar Technical School in nearby Spennymoor, said the lad as he held forth one lunchtime.

"There's one in Bishop Auckland called the King James the First Grammar School," chipped in the young Burton. "I wonder when he was chairman?" Several of the boys went away to think about that one. Perhaps the history master would know!

A fellow called Jack Dormand, born in Haswell Working Men's Club where his parents were the stewards, had been a pupil at Wellfield in the 1930s and had liked it so much that he returned as a teacher from 1940-48. He recalls that it was a very traditional grammar school where all of the teachers were university graduates and wore academic gowns.

Dormand himself was a Physical Education graduate from Bede College at Durham – as John would be later – and had worked his way up through the local Labour Party, serving on Haswell Parish Council and Easington Rural District Council before, against expectations, he received the nomination for the Easington Parliamentary seat. At the 1970 Election, he succeeded Manny Shinwell as the constituency's MP and within three years, he was made an assistant whip.

In Harold Wilson's Government of 1974-79, he was Senior Whip and Lord

Commissioner of the Treasury. His other official posts included a term as Secretary of the Northern Group of Labour MPs and then a Shadow Cabinet appointment as Chairman of the Parliamentary Labour Party.

In 1987, he was elevated to the House of Lords as a life peer, calling himself Lord Dormand of Easington – not bad for a Wellfield boy whose parents had run the local club.

John worked hard during his first two years at Wellfield but his abiding passion was sport. John looked forward to the annual Sports Day where he was one of the best sprinters for his age and regularly broke school records.

"I never bragged about my skills as an athlete," he says. "As far as I was concerned, they were a gift from God. I believed that then and I still believe it today. He gives us all skills but it's up to us how, why and when we use and develop them. Mind you, when I broke those tapes at the end of the hundred yards, or whatever the race was, I was very pleased with myself, chuffed to bits. I loved it when the other lads congratulated me on a good performance but I did the same for them when they cracked it."

His PE teacher, Bill Saunders, who later became Director of the Sports Council for the North-East, was his role model – in later life John too became a PE teacher because of Saunders' influence.

"He was a tremendous influence; quite simply, a lovely man," says John. "Hard, but with a heart of gold. There were times when we called him every rotten name under the sun but, really, we worshipped the ground he walked on."

Years later, when Burton was chairman of recreation on Sedgefield District Council and Saunders was directing the Sports Council, the two often met. "It was a good feeling, teacher and pupil working together," he says. "I wanted Bill to be proud of me and of what I'd achieved and I think he was. He was definitely one of my childhood heroes."

Strangely enough, when Tony and Cherie Blair were looking for a home in the area after the 1983 election, they found a likely house called Myrobella in Trimdon Colliery. Saunders was the executor for the family which was selling it.

When Saunders died, his wife, Carrie, asked John if the grammar school boys would carry the coffin at his funeral.

"There were so many who wanted to do it," says Burton. "How they all found out I just don't know. I had telephone calls from dozens, people I hadn't heard from since we'd all left school. Those who weren't selected for what was regarded as that great honour, to carry Bill to his final resting place, still turned up and, despite not being actual pallbearers, carried, instead, their memories on the day.

"I'll never forget it. All of us had recollections of Bill sending us on long runs, carrying above our heads one of those old, and very heavy, slatted gym benches.

They really were very heavy, and I mean heavy, even after a short time. There's a very long walk through St Paul's churchyard at Trimdon Colliery to the church itself, a very lengthy pathway."

The coffin was taken carefully from the hearse, the Wellfield team standing ready to receive it. As they hoisted the coffin onto their shoulders, all dressed in black suits with spotlessly white shirts and black ties, Saunders would have been impressed, and proud of them all.

"Right lads," Burton whispered, "twice round the cemetery and back."

They started to giggle. Bill would have seen the joke but would have roared: "Burton – behave yourself. Now!" When Carrie Saunders heard the story later, she was delighted and repeated it often.

The official sport at Wellfield was Rugby Union but soccer was also allowed, just as long as it did not interfere with the rugby. The school had an extremely good under-15 rugby team, of which Burton was a member, playing at fly-half or stand-off. Against all odds, they won the County Cup, beating Hartlepool in the final.

Saunders eventually gave permission for another master, 'Corker' Dobson, the woodwork teacher, to run a soccer team but only when no rugby was being played. Dobson watched all of his fledgling footballers very carefully and predicted that Burton would one day play for England.

Burton was a winger but always wanted in his heart of hearts to be a centre forward. He could play on both wings because, as he says, there being no Latin alternative available, he was "both-footed". He worked on this skill which proved valuable later in his soccer career.

The Wellfield football team joined the local league, based around Peterlee and Horden, and topped it easily with about a hundred goals for and seven against – "something of a whitewash". Dobson was reluctant to enter the County Cup but Burton is certain that, had he done so, they would have walked it. Some of the players went on to greater things: Ralph Ramshaw became a professional for Sunderland, Barry Storey played for Crook Town AFC and took part in an FA Amateur Cup Final at Wembley, a lad called Humphries joined Bowburn in the North-Eastern League, John Leather played in the Wearside League, George Corner was a Northern League player and Burton himself went on to do rather well in the game.

Perhaps another reason why the young boy found PE and sport so attractive was the PE mistress, Miss Richardson, who worked alongside Bill Saunders.

"She was a brunette," John remembers, "and absolutely gorgeous. All of the lads were in love with her and, in fairness, she did have the odd kind word for us, but that just made matters worse. I've seen two boys fighting over whether

Miss Richardson smiled at one of them or at the other. I was never smitten quite to that extent, but I think she did smile at me – once!"

By his own admission, Burton simply played his way through grammar school. Sport ruled his life; he was the fastest sprinter, he played tennis and basketball and, in the first two years, he found academic work easy.

In fact, the only time in the school year that he dreaded was the period leading up to the Christmas party. A special training course was necessary.

"In those days, much of this annual 'do' was taken up by Old Tyme Dancing," he recalls, "and so we all had to be taught to be fully proficient in our knowledge of the intricacies of such favourites of the time as the Veleta, the Military Two Step, the Gay Gordons (can you say that today and still be politically correct?), the St Bernard's Waltz, the Square Tango, the Circassian Circle and the Progressive Barn Dance.

"I liked that one because you got to dance with all the girls, albeit very briefly. We even learned a peculiar, but entertaining, number called the Mississippi Dip, performed to some of the hits of Al Jolson. Everybody worked up a sweat during that. Twice through and you were shattered!"

One thing that the 12-year-old Burton discovered during these dancing lessons was that girls were not the aliens he and his friends had, until then, believed them to be. For these embryonic excursions into the mysteries of dancing and human relationships, which is what they were, each boy was allocated a partner. John's was a girl called Lily Rutherford. All that he can really remember about her is that she could carry on a conversation while they moved around the floor, seemed to be a lot better at the Terpsichorean arts than he was and probably carried the bruises on her feet long afterwards to prove it.

"I like to think that I'd have been better at it if she hadn't chattered so much," he says.

Inevitably, though, there came a time when the halcyon days of youth faded and the schoolwork became harder. Much harder as John had failed to put in the groundwork.

He'd enjoyed geography with Bill Moyes, who went on to become an advisor to the Durham County Education Committee and was respected as a writer, primarily about local history, but too many lessons, he feels, were 'chalk and talk'. Pupils were compelled to take copious notes from the blackboard or from teachers' dictation. "Those people didn't teach," he says, "they simply imparted information."

In English literature lessons, Shakespeare was merely read around the class.

"You read the first 12 lines," they were instructed. "Then the next one will do the same."

John Burton: The Grit in the Oyster

John recalls: "Somebody could have been halfway through Shylock's great speech proclaiming his humanity or well into one of Macbeth's soliloquies, daggers and all, but at the end of 12 lines he had to stop and someone else took over. Nobody took any notice at all of the punctuation. It was dull, it was boring and it went on for lesson after monotonous lesson. The teacher kept telling us that Shakespeare was not dead nor ever would be. You could have fooled us. Shakespeare himself would have been bored had he been in our English group."

The day eventually arrived when he wanted to leave Wellfield, before taking his GCEs, but his father refused.

All of his friends in the year above him had taken their exams and were moving on. Jim Seymour had gone to be an apprentice draughtsman at Dorman Long in Middlesbrough, others had taken up training in the coal mines. John wanted to follow in their footsteps, to earn money himself. He felt, yet again, that he was being left behind.

Both John and his father were strong-willed and there were many arguments and discussions late into the night. Eventually Donald won the day. John would stay on at school and he is still grateful that his father was so stubborn.

But that decision proved to be the easy part of his fifth form year. Apart from his occasional bouts of bronchitis, John was never really ill and if he was feeling under the weather a bit he always brushed the ailment to one side. He never missed school with a cold or a tummy bug – they would have interfered with his sporting pursuits.

This time, however, something was decidedly different. For a few days, his ankles and knees felt sore. Even his hips hurt. Perhaps he had overdone things on the football field, gone in too hard on that tackle last Saturday? Then Tuesday came, and he shivered as he climbed down the steps of the school bus at the end of the day. His ankles would not bend properly; they were stiff and they hurt a lot. What on earth was the matter?

He struggled home for tea and began to prepare for his big night: he'd been picked for the first time to play for the school basketball team. After tea, he popped down to his friend Jim Seymour's house, and just as he was leaving to collect his kit bag, the pain in his legs became excruciating. To avoid anyone noticing, he bent down as if to tie his shoelace. When he was sure everyone was out of sight, he lurched over to the garden wall to hold himself upright. He could not stand by himself. Something was terribly wrong. Using walls and fences to support himself, he edged his way homewards. It took forever, he remembers. He could barely put one foot in front of the other.

Eventually, he arrived at his own door and, as he limped through it, he collapsed. The usual, cheerful, two-minute walk from Jim's house had become a feat of endurance, a daylight nightmare. "I just hoped that none of my pals had seen me," he remembers.

Once inside, the tears began and they would not stop. They fell for himself and for the pain, but primarily they fell for the awful realisation that he might never get another chance to represent the school at basketball and – worst of all – for the fact too dreadful to countenance that he would let down his team-mates.

"I wasn't a softie," he says, "but I'd never known pain like this. My mother knew me and my ways better than anybody and quickly realised that something was very wrong. I'd been in a few scuffles in my time but had never run home crying. Whether I won or lost a fight, I took it in good part, but this was unbearable pain, infinitely greater than a simple bloody nose."

Mrs Burton sent for the local doctor, Harbinson, who arrived within the hour. He walked straight in without knocking, as doctors did in those days, and found the boy on the sofa, perspiring heavily, shivering, tears streaming down his face. His mother had removed his scuffed black shoes and was praised by the doctor for having done so. Harbinson began his examination immediately and tutted to himself as he felt his way along John's legs.

"I've seen this before," he said when he did eventually speak. "It's rheumatic fever."

He had worked in the Far East and had seen the disease many times before – but not often in England.

He warned, though, that the period of convalescence was long, that John would have to be on his back for six months or longer and that he must not exert himself at all so that there would be absolutely no strain on his heart. Failure to carry out his instructions to the letter would almost certainly leave John with a heart weakness for the rest of his life.

However, he said, more hopefully, they had caught the thing early and, with luck and careful nursing, there might be little in the way of after-effects. Having written a prescription and, promising to return the following day, he left.

Dorothy Burton was extremely worried but tried not to let John see how she felt. Smiling, she leaned over him.

"Now then young man; you heard what the doctor said. Let's have you upstairs, into your pyjamas and into bed."

John did not complain and had to be helped up the stairs. Soon he was in bed and fast asleep, his pulse still racing.

His mother went downstairs and sobbed uncontrollably. When Donald came in from school, she hugged him and, between the tears, told him what Dr Harbinson had said. He poured himself a drink and sat down to take stock of the situation and of the consequences.

All sorts of things rushed through his head; John's future health, his schoolwork and GCEs, his sport, the burden on Dorothy were just some of them. He crept upstairs and looked into where his son was sleeping soundly. Kissing his clammy brow, he, too, fought back the tears. Then, telling Dorothy that he was popping out, just for a few minutes, he made his way slowly to the ancient church on the green.

After about two weeks, John did not feel so ill and, after three, wanted to be up and about but was told that he had to stay where he was, flat on his back. To pass the time, he read a lot and listened to the wireless. His father had rigged up an extension speaker from the set downstairs so that he could hear his favourite programmes but he also listened to a lot which had never appealed to him before. On the BBC there were the Light Programme and the Home Service but he was also addicted to Radio Luxembourg, which broadcast every evening. It was on this popular music station that he heard so much that would influence his own developing tastes. It was also a sponsored weekly programme on Luxembourg that first persuaded him to drink Ovaltine. A popular favourite during his convalescence was Dick Barton and he also became addicted to The Archers.

"It might have been 'an everyday story of country folk'," he says, "but they weren't like any country folk in the Trimdon area! Still, the storylines were good and I really did become an addict. If any of my friends were visiting while it was on, they had to be quiet. I'm sure they thought I'd become feeble-minded."

The visits by friends were an important part of John's gradual recovery.

"I think they must have had a secret rota. Never a day went by without one or more of them dropping in and there must have been times when they had so much homework to do but they never missed calling in. They were absolutely brilliant and I'm sure I wasn't always the best of company. Lying on my back for month after month was very frustrating and I did get short-tempered but I was definitely better on sunny days even though I knew that I couldn't go out.'

Donald and Dorothy also spent a lot of time with him.

"My Dad would sit in the room with me and mark books from school. He didn't need to say a lot. Just his being there was enough but he did take time to teach me to play Bridge. I don't think I was very interested at first; the rules were complicated and I took ages to get the hang of bidding. Sometimes, I just couldn't even be bothered. Then, one day, it all seemed suddenly to make sense and I couldn't wait for friends to call so that I could show them how to play. Funnily enough, it wasn't many weeks before the lads were absolutely rushing to our house to play the game. For me, it was a far cry from football but it was, in a peculiar way, a fascinating substitute. Bridge kept me sane at a time when I wondered if I would ever be able to kick a ball again and it tempered my frustration too."

Gradually, little by little, John was getting better but still observed carefully the restrictions placed upon him. He knew that he must not strain his heart if he was to live a full life eventually. Then, one day, something happened which was to speed his recovery and to baffle medical science.

His mother knew a man who would today be described as being into alternative medicine. His name was Lowson and he was from Hartlepool. He had been recommended to her by a friend when she had found a small lump in her breast. She went to see him, he prescribed some treatment and, in time, the lump disappeared. Dorothy believed it to be nothing short of a miracle and the lump never came back.

He had also cured a young Trimdon Village man of psoriasis when all the regular medical men had said that his condition was incurable. After Lowson's treatment, the ailment never returned.

Mrs Burton wrote to Lowson asking him to come to see John. She would pay his bus fares and his fees, she told him. A few weeks later, he arrived, talked for a long time to Mrs Burton and then examined the boy. He told her to carry on with Dr Harbinson's medication which had been prescribed but also to try some alternatives which he left with her. These were administered to John, precisely as instructed, and what had been a gradual recovery gathered unbelievable pace.

In the course of time, John was summoned to see a specialist called Dr Chalmers. He looked at the results of an ECG and said that he could not understand such a rapid recovery. John simply should not have been as healthy as the tests showed. They were repeated but still with the same results. A few more weeks of convalescence, he told Mrs Burton, and the lad could return to school.

Neither Lowson nor his herbal remedies were ever revealed to Drs Harbinson and Chalmers but, that summer, John Burton not only sat his GCE exams but also competed in the sprint events at Wellfield Sports Day. He was not the victor ludorum that year and he gained only three GCE passes but he had successfully climbed the mountain which only he, his parents and a herbalist had believed he could. As a matter of information, Lowson never charged the Burtons for his bus fares.

"I think it was after my recovery when I realised that life could throw up no challenge that I wasn't prepared to face head on," he says, "and I still think that my parents' prayers helped in no small way."

John elected not to go into the 6th Form at Wellfield. Instead, he enrolled for

GCE resits and Advanced Level GCEs at the Billingham campus of Stockton and Billingham Technical College. He achieved the GCEs but before he could actually take his A-levels, he decided to try a different course. He felt he was stagnating, that his progress was just too slow. He had already lost too much time and needed to move on.

Teacher-training was an option suggested by his father and the College of the Venerable Bede at Durham University seemed the obvious choice. It was now 1960, he was 19 and Donald had been a student there exactly 30 years before.

John was in no doubt that he should become a schoolteacher but he had no A-levels to support his application. Still, it was worth a try and there were other reasons why, he believed, Bede College might accept him. At the end of the day, life was, surely, about much more than simply paper qualifications! He had more strings to his bow.

4: The whirligig of time

UNCERTAIN of the outcome because of his lack of A-levels, John Burton wrote to Bede College in Durham City, applying for a place to train as a teacher.

To a degree of surprise, he received an invitation to an interview and was told to report to the college office. On the appointed day, still thinking he was an unlikely candidate, he put on his new charcoal-grey suit, mounted his red Vespa scooter and headed off for Durham City.

The drive from Trimdon Village, through Bowburn and Coxhoe, was pleasant enough and he wondered what the day had in store. He knew the city well but had never before been to Bede, and he had no idea who he was to meet nor what they might ask him.

The college was on Gilesgate. Next door was the ladies' teacher training college of St Hild's.

"Thank heavens I presented myself at the right one," Burton says. "They were remarkably alike in appearance and the signing was not particularly good but, in those days, it would never have done for a gentleman to be seen at Hild's outside 'visiting hours'."

As he walked towards the main entrance, he admired the beautifully-manicured lawns which sloped down towards the towpath and the River Wear. The imposing sandstone buildings were in a tranquil setting, cathedral and castle in the near distance where they had stood for almost 900 years.

Burton presented himself at the office some ten minutes before his appointment and was asked if he would mind waiting a moment or two. Even within those few minutes, he sensed that there was an atmosphere about the place: imposing, but warm and welcoming. Was it, perhaps, simply that he wanted so much to be part of this establishment which had turned so many generations of young men into quality teachers?

Before long, a secretary took him along winding corridors and stopped in front of a heavy, wooden door. She knocked and a deep voice answered.

"Come!"

She opened the door and said quietly: "Good morning Mr Webster; Mr Burton's here for his appointment."

Nobody had ever called him "Mr Burton" before. She ushered him into a large oak-panelled room and closed the door as she left. Almost everywhere there were books – shelf upon shelf of them.

Danny Webster got up from his chair, shook hands and introduced himself.

John Burton: The Grit in the Oyster

As Vice-Principal, he was one of the most senior members of the Bede staff. Everybody connected with the place had the greatest respect for Mr Webster; he was known to all simply as "Danny" but few, even other lecturers, called him that to his face.

The next half hour turned out to be not so much an interview but rather a friendly chat. Burton felt that Webster already knew him although they had never met. He had obviously spoken to the Rector of Trimdon, one of John's referees for a place at this Church of England college.

How was John's health now? How were his A-level studies going? What about his football? While another of the Durham colleges, Hatfield, shone in rugby, Bede was renowned as the 'football college'. How was his father nowadays, Webster wanted to know. He had come to Bede in 1930, had he not? John could not remember if he had mentioned this family link in his letter of application.

He answered all the questions and did not feel at all uneasy or overawed in the presence of this important man who would say yes or no to his application. Physical Education and History were the two subjects he wanted to study and it became clear from the conversation that Webster had previously discussed his application with the two heads of department concerned.

At the end of the 30 minutes, the lecturer ended the interview and sent John off to meet the PE and history men. They outlined the courses he had already read about in the college prospectus, and then invited him to stay for lunch. Two second year students took him to the dining room.

This was another new experience, totally unlike Wellfield or Billingham. The whole place vibrated to a magical symphony of sound; the loud chatter of young men, whispered conversations, laughter, the scraping of cutlery on crockery, exhortations to pass the condiments and chair legs moving across the polished floor. He had hundreds of questions which his hosts, as they ate, did their best to answer.

By the time the meal was over, he was more convinced than ever that Bede was where he needed and wanted to be.

As he rode home, he reflected on whether he had made a good impression. Had he said the right things? How long would it be before he heard anything from the college?

He did not have to wait long. Two days later, on his return from Billingham, there was a letter waiting for him. His mother, as anxious as he to know its content, urged him to open it quickly. After a moment's hesitation, he did so and the worried frown turned to a beaming smile.

"It says that there's a place for me at Bede in September and that my main subjects will be Physical Education and History," he told her. "They'll send

Top: John Burton with his mother, Dorothy, (left) and with his father, Donald. **Bottom:** Donald Burton (centre with pipe) and his cricketing fellows from Durham: Syd Milnes, George Moorse, Gilbert Heyes and Albert Rickett

Top: *The 1948 class of eight-year-olds at Trimdon Village Primary featuring John Burton on the far left end of the second row.* **Left:** *Burton in the 1956 AJ Dawson Grammar School U15 County Cup winners.* **Right:** *Durham cathedral from the grounds of Bede College and, below, the former college*

54

Top: John Burton with his Lambretta in 1960, and with his girlfriend Lily Darby at the 1961 Bede College Ball. *Bottom:* John and Lily's wedding at St Mary Magdalene Church, Trimdon, in 1963

Top*: John Burton, front row on the right, with the Stockton FC team in 1965-66 – the season he scored 75 goals and broke the Wearside League record.* ***Bottom****: Burton the young PE teacher with his football team at Albany Road Secondary Modern School, Stockton, in 1964-65*

Top: Burton's guitar accompanied him wherever he went – here on a 1963 Outward Bound course in Eskdale (left); in the 1970s, his moustache became similarly faithful. **Bottom:** Skerne in 1983 (left to right): Burton, Marshal Thomas, Gordon Dyke, Edwin Thomas and Brian Childs

Top: *Tony Blair campaigning in 1983 in Sedgefield with Coronation Street star Pat Phoenix and, behind, John Burton.* ***Bottom:*** *The new Sedgefield MP celebrates his first victory in 1983 with Mick Terrans, former leader of Durham County Council, on the left and George Ferguson on the right*

Top: *Skerne remember the 1882 Trimdon Colliery Disaster in 1989: John Burton, Edwin Thomas, Peter Brookes and Brian Childs perform before the local MP Tony Blair.* ***Bottom:*** *Burton as a councillor, in 1983 with an 8ft 4½in stinging nettle, and as mayor in 1987 on a bouncy castle*

*Top: Tony and Cherie Blair in their new house, Myrobella, in Trimdon Colliery in 1984 with their first child, Euan. **Left:** John Burton with Neil Kinnock, then the Labour Party leader, in 1987 when Burton was mayor of Sedgefield. **Below:** Burton at Myrobella with Kristin Johnsen, a Norwegian work experience pupil who worked at the constituency office at Myrobella*

Top: *Blair announces that he will run for the Labour leadership in Trimdon Labour Club in 1994.* **Bottom left**: *The mayor's footy skills fail to impress in 1987.* **Bottom right:** *John Burton leading a marching band in the 1970s.* **Facing page:** *Blair and Burton at Newbiggin, Northumbria, in 1996*

further details later but I'm to write back straight away if I want to accept the offer."

"And do you?" asked Mrs Burton.

"Mam!" he countered. "You do ask some daft questions."

She hugged him and he went to the table to write his acceptance. It was in the post before his father was home from school. The family had a lot to talk about that evening. John suddenly wanted to know everything about Donald's time at Bede and especially about the course he had followed. The older Burton did his best to answer but pointed out that this was 1960 and a lot would have changed in the 30 years since he was there.

A few weeks later, the promised information arrived from the College and John carefully read every single word of it. He was surprised at just how much PE clothing he was required to have; it read like a list of essentials for a pentathlete at the Olympic Games. Could his parents afford it? There was also a list of books he needed to buy; it was like a university library stock-check but without a Biggles anywhere in sight.

Another shock was the breadth of study he would have to undertake, particularly during his first year: the psychology of education, the sociology of education, the history of British education, health education, mathematics, general studies, English – and all of these on top of PE and History. By his own admission, he had played his way through school but now he was going to have to both play and work his way through university and strike a healthy balance between the two.

In doing so, he would be treading a well-marked path. Henry VIII and Oliver Cromwell had both tried to found a university in Durham, partly to challenge the duopoly of Oxford and Cambridge, but it wasn't until an Act of Parliament in 1832 that it was established. The teacher training college, originally called The Durham Training School for Masters, was set up seven years later, in 1839, as a Church of England establishment to train Christian young men as schoolteachers. It was renamed Bede College in 1886 and became the College of the Venerable Bede in 1936.

Having begun its working existence in 103, Framwellgate on October 4, 1841, the first buildings to be created specially for it were erected between 1845 and 1847; these were further extended at various times until 1858, the year in which St Hild's Teacher Training College for Ladies was established. Later additions date from 1875 and the mid-1950s. The beautiful college chapel, designed by Seely and Paget and described by Pevsner as "an outstanding work of modern ecclesiastical architecture", was built just before the outbreak of the Second World War.

John Burton: The Grit in the Oyster

The standard dress for Durham students in 1960 was a college blazer and tie, white shirt and grey flannels. To buy these, he travelled to the university outfitter, a large shop in Durham's Saddler Street, where the two elderly but dapper gentlemen who served him spoke in a most deferential manner: "Would sir be requiring the standard navy blue blazer? Much longer-wearing is this barathea one. We recommend it most strongly."

They would, of course. It was much more expensive but, John had to agree, it did look much better and had a more quality feel to it. He chose the barathea, despite the added cost, but would pay the difference himself rather than pass that expense on to his parents.

"When it comes to flannels, sir, we always advise at least two pairs."

These were salesmen of the first order. "Gentlemen out with friends for the evening have been known to be careless with their drinks!"

This was when it was not done to be seen out in jeans so two pairs it was. They failed to persuade him to buy two ties but he did purchase a Bede scarf; rather fetching, he thought, in light blue with darker blue stripes. Despite the temptation to do so, he resisted wearing that scarf until he actually started at Bede in the September but when his parents asked to see how he looked in the blazer and flannels he was happy to show them.

"I felt proud," John recalls, "but they were even more so. They were absolutely over the moon and that meant a lot to me. I think there'd been a time, when I had rheumatic fever, that they honestly believed that they'd never see this day nor a day like it."

Since he was within easy travelling distance of Durham City and had a scooter, John lived at home during his first year, a not uncommon practice. He had his lunch at Bede every day and attended the formal dinners on Thursday evenings but enjoyed home comforts for the rest of the time. For the previous four years, he had been courting a local girl, Lily Darby from Trimdon Colliery, after they had met at the weekly dance at nearby Deaf Hill.

As that first year passed, he realised that, although he had initially thought that he had the best of both worlds, he was missing out on a lot of college life. Things like the Saturday night dance did not bother him nor the get-togethers with the young ladies from St Hild's; he was more than happy with Lily. What he did miss were the nights in the bar with football and rugby colleagues, especially when they were celebrating a victory – he knew that he could not drink and then drive home. He decided that the next two years would have to be spent wholly at Bede even though he would then need special permission, an exeat, to go home for some weekends. Lily agreed that this was a sensible move.

Unlike the academic side of his school life, which he had not enjoyed at all, most of the lectures at Bede captured his imagination.

"Isn't it funny?" he considers. "Once I was there, I really wanted to learn. It was as if I'd been waiting for 20 years and, quite suddenly, the desire to learn became a hunger. The more I absorbed, the more I wanted to know. It was really as if I was almost putting on weight academically with every lecture I attended, every discussion group of which I was a part, every sporting activity in which I was involved. I became bloated not only with information and newly-acquired skills but, and this may sound odd but it's true, with a desire to pass on that knowledge, those skills to others.

"I couldn't wait to go on my first teaching practice and I really did think at that time that the world was waiting for my emergence as a teacher. My colleagues felt the same way. We had yet to realise the truth of the old adage that you can lead a horse to water but that you cannot force it to drink. Like thousands of trainee teachers before us, we were to learn this lesson the hard way but were better practitioners ultimately for having had to do so."

It was Danny Webster who gave John and his young colleagues the best advice any trainee teacher could ever receive. "You must never think, gentlemen," he warned, "that you will ever enter a classroom with the words 'you will respect me' tatooed on your forehead. You will never do so! If you want to gain the respect of your pupils, then you will have to earn it and the best way of doing so is by demonstrating that you also respect them and their rights, and by doing your preparation and marking thoroughly and by involving them actively in every lesson you take.

"If you fail to deliver what they expect, then you will fail in their eyes. Worse than that, you will have let them and yourself down. Mutual respect, I repeat gentlemen, is what teaching is all about."

Says Burton: "Before coming to Bede, Danny had long been a practising teacher and knew full well what he was telling us.

"The majority of our lecturers were very good and talked a lot of sense. They gave us every assistance to turn our ideas, our plans into practice. We might spend hours and days drawing up schemes of work and lesson plans for our teaching practices but if they were not up to the required standard then these gurus would put a red line through them, explain where they fell short or why they would not work and then send us away to start again from scratch.

"I can remember sitting at my desk, a barren sheet of paper in front of me, cursing a lecturer or tutor simply because I was sitting there and not enjoying a football practice or an evening in the bar with the lads. At the same time, and grudgingly, I knew that they were right and that I was wrong. There are no short cuts in teaching. You might as well do it right or simply not bother at all. At the end of the day, the kids will always find you out."

It was to be a philosophy that extended beyond his career into his politics. In the same way that children had to be involved in the lessons, so people had to be involved in the decision-making processes of the local Labour Party.

"If you keep people in the dark and feed them on a diet of manure," he argues, referring both to schoolchildren and voters, "you mustn't be surprised if you produce a population of mushrooms. Knowledge really is power and both knowledge and power are the right of the electors. Every politician worth his salt today should keep that fact, because it is a fact, firmly in mind at all times."

During his first week at Bede, Burton was walking along a corridor when George Smith, soon to become Vice-Principal, came round a corner and walked towards him. As they passed, Smith greeted him: "Good morning Mr Burton." They had never even met before and Burton, puzzling as he went on his way, wondered: "How on earth did he know me?" What Burton was soon to discover was that Smith, known to the students as "Ganges" because of his initials, GNGS, not only took great pride in knowing every single student by sight and by name but also had an encyclopaedic knowledge of their histories and interests. Following in Danny Webster's footsteps, he was held in both affection and esteem by the generation of Bede students which knew him. Burton learned that Smith made a point of memorising the photographs which all new students were required to send to the college before they started. By the time they arrived in person, he could identify them all.

"There was at least one occasion," John recalls with a wry smile, "when a large group of young men from Bede, some 20 or so, tumbled boisterously, much the worse for wear, out of a public house on Claypath. Who should just happen to be walking past but Ganges. We, yes I was one of them, hardly noticed him as he called 'goodnight gentlemen'. When we got up for breakfast the next morning, not feeling at all like doing so, each of us found a personal note pushed under the door of our room. Mine read: 'Good morning Mr Burton. I would be pleased if you could join me for coffee in my study at ten.' It was more a summons than an invitation and one that could not be ignored.

"Accordingly, at five minutes to ten, washed, shaven and extremely smart of appearance, as references used to put it, I presented myself at his door. I knocked, was called in and was amazed to see all of my companions of the previous night either standing or sitting shamefacedly around the room. Ganges was at his desk. 'Ah, Mr Burton, last but not least. Do come in and help yourself to coffee.' He then engaged in what can best be described as small talk for about a quarter of an hour. The expected admonishment never came, as such, but, as we started to leave, Ganges rose from his desk and quietly suggested:

'Gentlemen, may I congratulate you on your footballing victory yesterday and, further, you might like to consider on future forays into local hostelries sending out an advance party to check that the way is clear before disgorging your assembled mass into the street. Good morning gentlemen.'

"That was George Smith. To him, every Bede man was a gentleman, or would be before he left the college, but Smith was the most subtle and gracious gentleman of them all; he found time for everybody. Nothing to do with Bede was ever too much trouble for him. He was a lovely man."

During that first year, Burton became totally fascinated by the theory and practice of Physical Education. His studies in the subject were guided by Daf Hughes and Matt Tones. Tones was legendary among his students for announcing in lectures that he wished to make four points but he never got past three. Burton wonders whether if an examination question required a Bede student to comment on four aspects of something and he referred to only three he might still have gained full marks if he had written: "As with Mr Tones, the fourth point evades me for the moment."

Burton's time at Bede coincided with an educational revolution as younger tutors challenged the established order of teaching. The idea that just because something had always been done in a certain way, it should always be done in a certain way was no longer so readily accepted. Some people were daring to try something different.

The intake of 1960 was the first to be required to study for three years to gain a Certificate in Education, the passport to a teaching career. Until then, two years had been considered long enough. Even now Burton believes that the old two-year course was stretched out to three without anybody knowing quite how to fill the additional year. And so, during that last twelve months, he had only three lectures a week and those covered all subjects. Some of the remaining time was simply bulked out with extra PE sessions – the young sports-mad Burton was not going to object to that.

His first teaching practice, that watershed experience during, or after, which many a would-be teacher threw in the metaphorical towel, was in a school in Waterhouses, a small pit village near Durham City.

The children had failed the entrance examination to the local grammar school and had little motivation. "To be absolutely honest," says Burton, "they really did believe that, even at such a young age, they were already on the scrapheap. Their future, such as it was, offered very little. They'd end up with few, if any, qualifications and little hope of employment at the end of their schooldays which in those days was at the age of 15. Their junior school teachers had made it perfectly clear to them that if they didn't pass the scholarship then they were losers, nothing less."

Knowing this, Burton approached this practice in as positive a way as his young mind and heart knew. He was not going to teach 'losers'. These kids had to be in with a chance somewhere along the line; if they were not, then what was the point? Surely there had to be something going for them!

He was there for a few days to settle in before his Bede tutor, Jack Carrick, came to assess his progress, to see just how he was doing and how he was faring in the classroom. Was he 'up to it'? Did he have 'what it takes'?

The Maths lesson, 'sums' to the children, was going well when Carrick arrived and sat down quietly in an empty desk at the back of the class. Burton, aware that this first observed lesson would focus on his preparation, bearing, appearance and delivery of the subject matter, was determined to be nothing less than perfect. His file of lesson plans lay open on the teacher's desk in front of him. Surely nothing could go wrong. Could it? He remembered the famous phrase about never working with animals or children. He was on his guard. Carrick had been training teachers for a long time and would be sure to spot the slightest faults.

The topic of the lesson was cancelling out fractions and Burton was confident about what he was teaching. He had put a fraction on the blackboard and arrived at the stage where all that was left was '1 x 2'. Just one simplifying step was required to leave the correct answer, a whole number.

"Right then," said Burton, pointing to a sleepy-looking boy just across the aisle from where Jack Carrick was sitting. "All we need to do is to multiply one by two. So then, what's the answer? One times two?"

There was silence. The boy continued to look sleepy and did not respond. Burton felt uneasy. Surely it was a simple enough calculation! The success or failure of his teaching practice rested on this lesson. He tried again.

"Look. Think of it another way. Imagine that I have two apples in one hand; that's one lot of two apples. How many apples do I have?"

Still no answer. The ensuing silence became deafening. Burton felt panic setting in.

"Alright then," he tried. "So what's two times one?"

When there was still no answer, Jack Carrick leaned across to the boy's desk and whacked him hard across the ear.

"Don't just sit there, lad," he shouted, his nose a mere inch from the boy's. "Answer the man."

"Two, sir," came the swift reply.

"There now, wasn't that easy?" Carrick beamed at the boy who cupped his ear which hurt considerably less than his pride.

Burton was genuinely shocked by his tutor's action but gratified, nevertheless, by the result.

"Well done," he said, and moved on to the next fraction.

There were no more silences for the rest of the lesson, nor, indeed, for the rest of his time at the school. The jungle drums had sent out the telling message: "Don't mess with Burton."

When Carrick next saw Burton, he apologised for having intervened in a lesson he had been there merely to observe but hoped he had been of some help. Burton conceded that his intervention had been both timely and helpful. Afterwards he reflected that the psychology of education lectures which were part of his course had offered interesting solutions to similar problems but that Carrick's instant cure had, equally, been more than effective.

A regular occurrence at Bede in those days was a lecture delivered to the whole college by an invited outside speaker. One of these, and they were always of a religious or inspirational nature, was delivered by a guest from the chemical company ICI. These talks were often excellent but the subject matter of this one, something to do with religion and metaphysics Burton remembers, was way over the heads of the students.

As they left the lecture theatre, having politely applauded the guest speaker, and moved to the studies of their personal tutors for a follow-up discussion, the vast majority confessed that they had found the talk difficult to comprehend. Burton's tutor was a scientist called Garnham. The discussions always followed the same format in that the tutor selected one student to offer his opinion and then the other members of the group were invited to make their contribution. Burton was well-versed in listening to the others and then airing his views when asked to do so, picking up on the previous speaker's main point. On this occasion, however, it all went wrong when Garnham asked him what he had thought of the lecture.

"To be absolutely honest," he told Garnham, "I don't have a clue what the gentleman was talking about."

There followed what seemed to be the longest silence he had known in his life before Garnham acknowledged, and not reluctantly, that he had not understood the content of the lecture either. The group went on to spend the remainder of the tutorial discussing sport!

Burton contends that it was this incident which taught him that, no matter what the consequences, honesty is always the best policy. To this day, if he does not understand something then he says so.

"It's always better to be enlightened by somebody else than to remain in the dark," he maintains.

John Burton: The Grit in the Oyster

The students at Bede studied steadily but academia was not the be all and end all of their lives. Their tutors and lecturers did not require such a commitment as they knew that such young men had other interests too. Burton worked on his sporting weak points, one of which was swimming. He reasons that he had footballer's legs and really couldn't swim well at all. One of his lecturers had told him that some of the best lessons result from the teacher having initial difficulty with the subject. Burton feels he became a good swimming teacher because, he says, he could relate to the children's fears of, and difficulties with, the idea of being in and moving in water. He also knew very well that not all children loved sport as he did, often simply because they believed that they were not very good at it, usually because somebody, peer or teacher, had told them that they were not.

"If you tell a child something often enough and forcefully enough," he says, "then the child will come to believe it. You can tell a child who's a potential sporting star that he or she just doesn't have what it takes and, while the odd one will be spurred on just to prove you wrong, the majority will take your word for it and give up. That's something that applies to every subject and aspect of life, not just to sport. I've heard former colleagues tell children that they're thick or stupid. Nobody should ever be allowed to say that to a child, not ever. They really do come to believe it and to act as they believe a thick person should. They become, in fact, self-fulfilling prophecies."

Burton also remembers one particular boy he taught at Sedgefield, a very intelligent young man who was little short of a genius at science.

"To be truthful, he'd never seemed very keen on PE and one day I was teaching him and his class how to do the long jump; 17 pace run-up, sprint as fast as you can, hit the board, rocking action, heel, toe, high knee, get your arms up and so on. This lad's body language screamed at me that he was bored mindless and totally disinterested in what we were doing. Still, when his turn came he ran up to the board and succeeded in jumping about a metre, if that. I suggested to him that surely he could do better next time if he put in just a bit more effort. His reply wasn't meant to be impolite, and I didn't take it as such, but he just looked at me and said quietly: 'Quite frankly Mr Burton, I can't see the point of it.'

"I thought for a moment before agreeing with him that there really wasn't a lot of point. When I asked him what he'd like to do instead, he replied that he'd like to try badminton so I sent him off to the gym to do just that. Before he left the school, he'd joined a badminton club and gradually became a tolerably good player. What's more, he found a sport that he enjoyed. But the point of the story is that he wasn't made to look silly in front of his friends, and he could've been very easily; rather he was allowed to enjoy sport and exercise but not forced to go in the particular direction that I was advocating."

As part of the Physical Education course, Burton was sent on an Outward Bound course in Eskdale in the Lake District. Also taking part in the same training were some young apprentices, including a 15-year-old lad called Fox who lived in London. Burton was amazed to hear that he had never seen a real cow in the countryside.

At the end of the course, he returned to a snow-covered Durham, a Christmas card landscape. He joined his old friends for an evening drink – or two, or three, or maybe more, at one of the city pubs. The merry group made its meandering way back along the towpath beside the River Wear to Bede, taking three or four times longer than usual for this short journey, partly as a consequence of the deep snow but also because they paused every now and then to render a verse or two of one of the popular songs of the day. These were interspersed with the odd rousing, if slightly slurred, rendition of such hallowed rugby songs as Little Angeline and one about the complicated physical, albeit legendary, relationship between a camel and the Sphinx.

As they came alongside Baths Bridge, the Burton party turned left up the side of the college and then sharp right into its grounds. They knew that they had to be quiet when passing the Principal's house but, while attempting to silence one another, they made even more noise, particularly when one of their number realised that he had lost one of his shoes and all had to retrace their steps until they found it.

The second passing of the Principal's house was marginally quieter but they then needed to cross the expansive lawn, more akin to a field, which would take them to the New Block in which they all had rooms. In the middle of this lawn was a hallowed war memorial, a carved obelisk topped with a cross. Around it was a low wall about two feet high. Beside this landmark, Burton brought the group to a wobbling and rather uncertain halt. Turning to Barry Mason, he bragged that, having been on the Outward Bound course, he could easily climb up and touch the top of the cross. Mason was inclined to disagree with him and voiced that opinion loudly. Again there was a lot of shushing from the others. Voices were lowered but Burton stuck to his boast as the snow continued to fall in large flakes.

However, before he could begin his ascent to prove his point, Mason beat him to it and soon reached the top of the monument, crooking his fingers over the upper part of the cross and heaving himself even higher.

As he did so, there was a sharp sound like the snapping of a branch from a tree. To their horror, and to Mason's, they realised that the cross had become

John Burton: The Grit in the Oyster

detached from its pillar and was falling towards the snow on the ground. The consequences could well have been tragic but, as he fell, Mason had the presence of mind to push himself away from the cross which landed just inches away from him.

After a moment of stunned silence, the entire group, still unsteady on their feet, attempted to flee the scene as fast as they could, forgetting about the stone wall, completely covered by snow, around the memorial. All fell flat on their faces before, like the Keystone Cops, picking themselves up and hurrying back to their rooms. They agreed that they would deny all knowledge of the incident and would not breathe a word of their escapade to anyone.

The next day at lunch, an announcement was made to the assembled student body that because of the strong winds during the previous night, and, no doubt, since it had been there for a good number of years, the cross on the war memorial had been dislodged and would be repaired as soon as the weather became more clement. The reprobates remained silent about their involvement, fearing that they would be sent down if it were ever discovered.

Because of Burton's Outward Bound experience, he was the first to be consulted by his peers whenever assignments on that topic were demanded. At the end of a lecture on Organising Active Camping Holidays for Young People, the members of his group were given two weeks to plan just such a visit; where would they go, what equipment and supplies would they need, what activities would they include, what ratio of staff to children would they stipulate? These and dozens of other factors had to be carefully considered by the Bede students who had not taken notes during the lecture and had been surprised when this task was set. Where could they turn for help? Who would have even a rough idea of the answers? John Burton suddenly found himself the unexpected focus of attention and the recipient of numerous free drinks. He was the Guru of Outward Bound. He had the answers.

He was perfectly happy to answer all of the questions but was so busy helping the others that he woke one Thursday night in a cold sweat, realising that the essay had to be handed in the next morning and that he had completely forgotten to write it. He leapt out of bed at three in the morning and worked frantically until ten, even missing his breakfast, to cobble something together. He read it through; it was disjointed, lacked detail and was, by his own admission and standards, a pathetic piece not worthy of submission. Rather than place it on the table near the lecture room door for marking, he consigned it to the waste paper basket, prepared himself for the forthcoming chastisement, and went to lunch.

Fourteen days later the assignments were returned, marked with appropriate comments. The lecturer made sure that everyone knew how everyone else had done.

"Mr A, a good attempt, although rather lacking in detail. Mr B, not bad, but I'd like to have seen some costings. Mr C, how could you take the group rock climbing when you lack the necessary certificates of competence?"

The grades were awarded; C, B, C and so on. Burton waited for the inevitable F for failed.

Towards the end of the session, the lecturer cleared his throat and broadcast to the group: "Gentlemen, you may like to know that I have awarded Mr Burton's assignment an A grade. It was a quite brilliant piece of work, for which I commend him. I am keeping his assignment as an exemplar to those who follow in your footsteps. You would all do well to copy his example."

Had the lecturer guessed that Burton's knowledge had been widely plagiarised – or had he just lost the file? To this day, Burton is still not sure.

With all the work, sport and, of course, the social life, John Burton's three years at Bede sped by.

By the time he left, his red Vespa scooter had been replaced by a motor bike, a Matchless 350, and as he rode it home from college for the last time he reflected on his student days. Where had the time gone? He thought about his friends and the lecturers. Would he see them again? Of course, they had all pledged to stay in touch and to meet up frequently but he knew that they were all embarking on a new stage in their lives and that new commitments would demand their time.

He was fiercely proud of having been part of the great institution which was the College of the Venerable Bede. He thought about the pride with which he and the others had worn its blazer, scarf and tie. He had been far from immature when he first walked through those college doors but the place itself and the life he had experienced there had made him into a young man ready to take on the world. It had been an important part of his life, something he would always remember and cherish.

No challenge now seemed too great; no obstacle would stand in his way. Nothing would prevent John Burton of Trimdon from making his mark on the world.

5: Those that do teach

IT WAS the early summer of 1963 and the newly-qualified teacher of Physical Education, John Burton, had already visited several County Durham secondary schools in his search for employment. But all the schools he saw had the same drawback: no dedicated gymnasium.

In all of them, during bad weather, indoor PE lessons had to stop when the gym, which doubled as the school hall, was transformed into the dining room. Even worse, in Burton's opinion, the children who were supposed to be doing PE at that time of the day were expected to set out the tables and chairs, and the first class after lunch had them all to stack away again before their lesson could begin.

While this was most definitely physical exertion, it was not his idea of physical exercise. Nor, he supposed, were the children very keen on the practice.

His standards were too high, his father told him. If he went on like this, he said, he would never find employment; he should lower his sights. The younger Burton, however, adamantly refused. His father had persuaded him to train as a teacher, he argued, and he had done so. He had spent three years learning how to implement the latest teaching techniques and to use the most modern equipment and was not now prepared to put all of that aside to spend time every day erecting dining facilities. Somebody had to do it, he readily agreed, but that somebody was not going to be John Burton. Would a History or English teacher cut short a lesson by 20 minutes every day to bring a class to the hall to do so? No, he maintained, and neither would he. So he cast his net further afield.

He scanned the education press and found, eventually, what looked like a decent prospect in the Hertfordshire town of Hoddesdon, some four miles from Hertford itself. He had never heard of the place but still submitted an application to Stanstead Road Secondary Modern School. This was indeed a venture into a brave new world for a lad who had travelled around the country in his youth but who had never lived outside the North-East of England.

When a letter arrived inviting him to attend for interview, Burton was pleased. He was attracted by the information the school had sent him and was determined to "go for it". Should his interview prove successful, friends and family would have to be left behind but they could be visited in the holidays – and there was always the telephone. It was not as if, he reasoned with all who questioned his plans, he was moving to the moon. Lily, whom he had courted since he was 15 and was to come with him as his new bride, was not so sure about that!

Burton arrived for the interview and was impressed with what he found. Hoddesdon was extremely attractive and the school certainly came up to his expectations. This was the job he wanted.

Before the interview, as he wandered around parts of the town, he felt himself stepping back in time. Down the centuries, wealthy traders had built themselves town houses here and many of their black and white, half-timbered dwellings dating back hundreds of years still survived. King Henry III had granted Hoddesdon a weekly market as well as an annual "fare" in 1253 and by the 18th Century the place had developed into an important coaching centre. More than 30 local inns had then serviced the Cambridge to London route.

This must have been a prosperous time since the renowned highwayman Dick Turpin regularly held up coaches on the Hoddesdon to Ware road before meeting his ignominious end on the gallows in York.

At the job interview, it soon became obvious that only two of the candidates were in with a chance: John himself and a man trained at the famous Loughborough College, renowned for the quality of the PE teachers it produced.

As it transpired, John was the successful candidate, possibly, he reasons, simply because he was known to be an excellent footballer and had even played in a trial for Bishop Auckland Amateur Football Club whose reputation in the sporting world was then legendary. His other qualities and skills had certainly been recognised and acknowledged but his association simply with the name of Bishop Auckland AFC had enhanced his credentials.

"Everybody had heard of their greatest player, Bobby Hardisty," he recalls, "sadly no longer with us now. They remembered the great Wembley clashes in the FA Amateur Cup between Bishop Auckland, the 'Two Blues' as they were always known, and the likes of Crook Town. What wouldn't we have given to have been in one of those Amateur Cup finals! They were the glory days of English amateur soccer." John was later to play for "The Bishops" on a regular basis.

During the holidays, before he started work in Hoddesdon, John and Lily were married in Trimdon Village at the ancient parish church of St Mary Magdalene which, although they did not know it at the time, was destined to continue to play a very important part in their lives. Acting as best man was one of John's childhood friends, Chris Alderson. They had met through the church and both were avid canasta and whist enthusiasts.

The wedding reception was in the Community Centre in the village but by then Lily was wishing that they had simply eloped. Everybody meant well; family and friends had worked together on the catering and the decoration of the church; in fact there was far too much to eat and drink and the noise and general fuss at the post marital festivities was all a bit too much.

Lily whispered to John: "Can't we just slip away quietly? Nobody would notice!" It was a forlorn hope, and it would be several busy hours before they were able to travel to Durham station to take the train south for their honeymoon.

"Looking back," says John, "it was a memorable day, a happy time and we were grateful to everybody who made it so but we just wanted a bit of peace."

They spent their honeymoon in York where both were highly embarrassed when, as they put down their borrowed suitcase at the hotel reception desk, confetti spilled like unseasonal snow from their clothes. They thought that they had removed it all but left a trail right up to their room.

On their return to Trimdon, they stayed with John's mother while preparing for their departure to what Lily continued to regard as "the other end of the country". She freely admits that, unlike John, she had not travelled much and Hoddesdon did seem a very long way from County Durham. They even found time to go on the annual church outing to the Northumbrian seaside resort of Whitley Bay where Lily was quite upset when the women in the group went off for a cup of tea and to look after the children while the men headed off in the opposite direction.

For their next visit to Durham station they travelled on John's motor bike, loaded with what they felt they would need to start married life in a new home. The bike was stowed in the guard's van and the train took them to London. With them was one item which was to go for many years wherever they went. It was a pedal bin in which they had packed some of their wedding presents and it proved to be a handy 'suitcase' whenever they moved house.

"It seemed to have a lot of significance in our lives at the time," he recalls, "but I couldn't for the life of me tell you where we parted company with it. It's a funny thing but we don't even have one in our kitchen today."

On the journey from London to Hertford, the newly-weds were again parted since John was for some unaccountable reason required "by the regulations" to travel in the guard's van with his motor bike. Lily, in the carriage, was not best pleased!

The school had found the newly-weds a flat in the attic of a public house in Hertford. It had not been used as accommodation for a lot of years and did not even have a door on it. On their first night there, they climbed into bed and John turned to Lily to say how wonderful it was that they had a place of their own, their first little home. Then it happened; the legs of the bed went straight through the floor! The next morning no amount of telling and retelling of the incident could convince their landlord that they had been having nothing more than an innocent chat...

Understandably, Mr and Mrs Burton were soon ready to move home. Their new digs were in the local vicarage as tenants of the Reverend Gandon and his wife. John played football, and soon he and Lily became as heavily involved with the church as they had been at home.

John's attitude to the actual act of worship had been greatly influenced by one of the Trimdon clergy, Father Riley, a member of the 'high church' Oxford movement. He had come from South Shields and had quickly built up a large, regular congregation which was enthralled by his style and by the content of his sermons. When the Burtons arrived at the Hoddesdon church, they found a complete difference. The services there were 'low church' and they practised something called north end communion which was totally alien to them. John and Lily breezed in on their first visit, genuflecting to the altar and crossing themselves in the high church way. The vicar was not at all surprised by this but some of the parishioners thought that they were Roman Catholic and might possibly attempt to change their church's ways, particularly since they were in such close contact with their incumbent at the vicarage.

It was also at Hoddesdon that John and Lily first started to visit a folk club in a local pub. Folk music and skiffle were just becoming very popular and it was there that John first heard the song The Trimdon Grange Explosion. Although he knew the story of the terrible pit disaster and had heard the poems about it, the song was new to him. He soon discovered that it had been recorded on the Topic label by Johnny Handle, a member of the Northumbrian group The High Level Ranters (the High Level being a famous bridge over the River Tyne between Newcastle and Gateshead), and he immediately went out and bought a copy.

At the folk club, the Burtons saw and heard performers they still regard as the forefathers of the folk movement, people like Alex Glasgow, Alex Campbell and Enoch Kent who travelled up to Hoddesdon from London. Until attending the folk club, John had only ever sung and played such music at Parent Teacher Association concerts to raise funds for the school. He looks back on those days now and cringes at the thought of how badly his self-taught guitar-playing must have been. Like so many of his contemporaries, as a child he had been badgered into learning the piano but had forsaken the ivories in his teens when the guitar had seemed so much more fashionable – and, indeed, much more portable.

The Burtons stayed at Hoddesdon for one enjoyable year and returned to the North-East because Lily was pregnant. She wanted to have her first baby in hospital but was told that there would be no beds available when the time came. Donald Burton was asked to find them somewhere to live nearer to home while they tidied up loose ends in Hertfordshire. Donald scoured estate agents in Stockton-on-Tees, about ten miles from Trimdon, where John had been appointed as a PE teacher at Albany Road Secondary Modern School.

Once he had found a likely address – the former home of Middlesbrough footballer Joe Scott in Darlington Lane which had a wonderful garden – Donald helped with the deposit, and once they moved in, he was a regular visitor, always happy to reminisce and enjoy a drink with his son at the nearby Mile House pub.

A bed had been arranged for Lily at the Hardwick Hall Maternity Hospital, now a hotel, just outside Sedgefield and in September 1964 she gave birth to their daughter Caroline.

"I was allowed to deliver Lily to the main door but wasn't allowed into the building," remembers John. "She and her suitcase were swept inside by the duty matron and then the huge front door was virtually slammed in my face. The place seemed like one of those German castles converted to a prison camp that you see in war films. Those were the days when men weren't encouraged to be there at the birth, in fact their presence was strictly taboo. I must admit, however, that when I went to see our new baby the staff were as nice as ninepence and she was gorgeous."

Their son Jonathan was also born there in March 1966.

A couple of months later, at the age of 57, Donald died of cancer. His death was not unexpected, but for John a lifelong friend and confidant had been taken from his life.

"As the years had passed," he says, "we'd developed the sort of father-son relationship that most can only dream of."

John and Lily paid ever more frequent visits to his mother Dorothy in Trimdon Village and eventually decided that it would be for the best if they sold up in Stockton and moved into 14, West Lane with her.

"It was a bit crowded in that West Lane house but we managed fine," says John. "And you see, the funny thing is that fate, or something, intervened in my life to draw me back again to Trimdon. It was as if building blocks were being put in place; I really do believe that. Lily and I never had the remotest intention of moving back. Nothing could have been further from our thoughts. We loved the Stockton house – even though I've never been a great gardener."

Before too long, it became clear that the extended Burton family needed more space and so they bought 7, West Lane, just along the street. It was a house John already knew well since one of his childhood friends had grown up in it.

"Leaving the old house with all of its memories was a terrible wrench," says John, "especially for my mother, but we'd reached the stage where all of us had to have more room, personal space if you like, and she understood the need for that. We were all getting on very well but, to be honest, we were falling over one another, sometimes literally, far too often."

Both John and Lily felt they had "come home". Lily had been raised in nearby Trimdon Colliery; her mother, Florrie, had been an invalid for most of her life and her father, Jack, had had to retire early following an accident down the coalmine.

This sense of homecoming was strengthened when John, having taught for two years in Stockton, was appointed Head of PE at Trimdon Village Secondary Modern School. He also took over his father's former role as secretary to the Parochial Church Council and, having given the matter a lot of thought, walked into Trimdon Working Men's Club one day and joined the Labour Party.

He still found time for football. Coaching school teams and his own footballing career went hand in hand, and continued to do so when he was appointed to the vacant Head of PE post at nearby Sedgefield Secondary Modern. It "went comprehensive" about a year later and was where John would remain for the rest of his teaching career until his early retirement on health grounds in 1994. Although he had to teach many different sports, football remained his favourite and he devoted hundreds of hours outside of school time to supervising schoolboy matches. Under his tutelage, Sedgefield Comprehensive won the Durham County Schools' Cup for four successive years.

"As any PE teacher will tell you, it's part of the job; it goes with the territory as it were but there was more to it than that," John says. "I'd learned a lot through being a schoolboy footballer myself. I'd seen how hard my teachers had worked with us and I firmly believed, and still do, that it was my duty to give something back to the game's grass roots. I was a fully-qualified coach and feel that I was able to motivate and inspire my lads to play well both as individuals and as members of a team. Some of them, like Colin Cooper of Middlesbrough, went on to play professionally and dozens of others did well locally, but even those who packed it in when they left school had learned incredibly valuable lessons about being team players and wanting to put in all the effort necessary to be a useful and crucial part of the winning team, not just in sport but in life generally.

"A lot of people still don't realise that a lot of the principles, standards and values so essential to team games can be transferred directly to make living day to day in every walk of life much easier, more meaningful and much more rewarding."

Grahame Parnaby was one of those who took part in the County Coaching Courses that John ran at what was then Middleton St George College, now part of Teesside International Airport. His brother David, now the director of the

John Burton: The Grit in the Oyster

Football Academy at Middlesbrough Football Club which nurtures young players, also took part.

"We looked up to and respected John for a number of reasons," says Grahame. "He was an excellent coach who set us achievable, if sometimes challenging, targets. Even when he needed to be critical, he always gave positive feedback to everyone but if he thought any of us wasn't giving 100 per cent he soon let us know. Even then he did it in a quiet way. He didn't ever humiliate anybody in front of their peers.

"We knew that, as a footballer, he was one of the best, a team player and a prolific goalscorer. I always remember that he gave the impression of having a kind of deceptively lazy or laid back approach – in other words he was a typical striker."

After a hard week's training, John's pupils would often come to watch him play at the weekends. He says: "Sometimes, above all the well-meant banter from the crowd and the occasional screams of derision, I'd hear a high-pitched voice or two urging: 'Come on sir; you can do it', or the slightly more irreverent: 'What's the matter Burton? Not tired already, are you?'. And there were times when such encouragement, often during a really hard match on a cold, wet, muddy and windswept pitch, was worth its weight in gold. That really is true, honestly."

Football has been an integral part of Burton's life ever since he was a member of the Trimdon Junior School team. In his heyday in the 1960s, the local, amateur leagues in which he competed were as important to the ordinary man in North-East villages as the performances of the professionals in the big cities – and many in the mining community did not have the cars or the money to make the journey to Middlesbrough, Newcastle or Sunderland.

It is perhaps difficult to comprehend today how much community support there was for the likes of Crook Town and Bishop Auckland Amateur Football Clubs. No self-respecting supporter, club scarf tucked proudly under overcoat collar to combat the chill terrace winds, would have dreamed of missing a local derby whatever the weather. Thousands would pack the grounds and whole families went along. Weddings were arranged around the local club's football fixtures. If Crook Town were playing Bishop Auckland at the Bishops' Kingsway Ground on a Saturday afternoon, then Crook would be like a ghost town and vice versa.

The stars of such teams really were "local heroes" and lifting the FA Amateur Challenge Cup at Wembley Stadium was the ultimate achievement. Bishop Auckland had been in the final a record 18 times and had won it on ten occasions – another record. Their first appearance was in 1896, the third year of the tournament, when they had beaten The Royal Artillery, Portsmouth 1-0. Crook Town's first final, in 1901, was against King's Lynn who they defeated 3-0 in a replay. It was not until 1949 that the final was regularly played at Wembley Stadium and in the early 1950s crowds of more than 100,000 were not uncommon.

1954 was the only year in which Crook ever met Bishop Auckland in the final and even then, after two drawn games, there had to be replays before Crook finally won a famous 1-0 victory.

After 1974, when the term 'amateur' had ceased to all intents and purposes to have any real meaning, the FA Amateur Challenge Cup was replaced by the FA Challenge Vase but, somehow, the magic of the glory days had gone.

John's amateur career had started when he was sought out at the age of 15 to play on the left wing for Fishburn Juniors on Saturday afternoons. During his time there, his team won the Lady Eden Cup, beating Browney in the final. Rheumatic fever interrupted his time with Fishburn but he has happy memories of playing there alongside Gordon Jones who went on to play for Middlesbrough and England.

At 17, he was recruited from Fishburn by Trimdon Grange to play in a team that included Tony Knox, who eventually played left back for England Amateurs. They were in the Wearside League, which was semi-professional, but John was still an amateur and so payments were technically illegal. However, John received £1.50 per week to cover his travelling expenses and, in a bid to keep him, Fishburn Juniors had offered an additional seven shillings and sixpence – a sum unheard of at the time.

From Trimdon Grange, in the year before he went off to Bede College, John played centre forward for Bowburn in the North Eastern League.

When he did arrive at Bede, he was suffering from an ankle injury which prevented him from playing football but, perversely, did allow him, during his first months there, to play centre at rugby, not his favourite sport but one which kept him fit while he awaited, impatiently, his return to soccer.

When that time came, he played in the Durham and District League for a Bede football team which also included the college Senior Man at full back – Jack Cunningham, later the MP for Copeland who served in the Cabinet in Blair's first term of office as Cabinet Office Minister. Games were played every Wednesday and Saturday, although the Wednesday side was far stronger as it included Bede men who played for Northern League teams on Saturdays. Bede's greatest rivals were Hatfield College who excelled at rugby but were always trounced by Bede at football.

John himself played some games for Cornsay Park in the Durham Central

League and, during one of them, received a piece of advice he remembers even now; on a bitterly cold Saturday, he was running down the right wing when one of the opposing team's big full backs, coming towards him with the ball, hit it for all he was worth. It struck John in the most delicate part of the male anatomy and he slumped, almost on the touchline, winded and feeling very sick, to the frozen ground.

Just above him, a man in his seventies leaned forward and said: "Come on, young feller, get up. Force yourself to pass water and the pain'll pass at the same time. Honest – it will."

John left the pitch in agony and struggled with his task; when, eventually, he completed it, almost miraculously the pain disappeared within seconds. It was advice which he has passed on to others countless times and which has proved to be an unfailing remedy for what he calls "a sudden blow to one's masculine pride".

The incident also reinforced for him something his father used to say: "Whenever anybody offers you advice, always listen to it. You don't have to take it but listen to what's being said and then make up your own mind."

When the Burtons arrived in Hertfordshire, John played for Hoddesdon Town Football Club in the Spartan League. During his only season there, both Wycombe Wanderers and Walthamstow Avenue wanted to sign him but it was not to be.

On his return to the north, he played briefly for Shildon AFC who reached the final of the County Cup but then he was signed by Stockton, the town where he and Lily were then living. As well as playing for the county while he was there, he broke the Wearside League setting a record with 75 goals in one season – a record which will stand forever since the league no longer exists. During his time with Stockton, they beat Herrington 10-0 with Burton contributing five.

His next move was to Billingham and during his season with them he was working towards becoming the youngest person to hold the Football Association's full coaching badge. The following season, Ferryhill Athletic took him on as player/manager but never allowed him to field the team nor to play the tactics he wanted. He had gone there at the committee's invitation, but encountered little apart from interference and obstacles from some of the very people who had been so desperate to use his skills. He was trying to play what was then the new 4-2-4 system; this required players accepting change, fulfilling roles that John believed they had shown an aptitude for, but instead the committee insisted on picking a team using the traditional 2-3-5 line-up.

This resistance to change and the challenge of dealing with it effectively was very frustrating at the time, but it would stand John in good stead when he encountered it again and again in his political career. He could see that because these people were putting money into the club they felt that they had a right to have a say in the team, but when his choices were constantly overruled, week after week, he was left with no option other than to resign.

"There was simply nothing to be gained by staying," he remembers, with a little bitterness. "They wanted me to do a job. They defined that job. They specified, perfectly clearly, the parameters within which I would have to work, and I did, but then, if you'll pardon the pun, they kept on moving the goalposts. Eddie Bell, the club secretary, pleaded with me to stay on the grounds that things would change but I'd had enough so I took my ball home, as we say in Durham!"

He had much happier experiences during his time with West Auckland in 1968. While he was playing outside-left there, the club reached the quarter-finals of the FA Amateur Cup, a major achievement. West Auckland had actually reached Wembley, just once, in 1961, only to be beaten 2-1 in the final by Walthamstow Avenue.

"There's one remarkable thing about West Auckland Football Club," John says, "which seems to be very little known but is an indisputable fact and it's a wonderful story. West Auckland really did win the first football World Cup in 1909, 21 years before the Jules Rimet Trophy was begun in 1930. What happened was that Sir Thomas Lipton, a famous and extremely wealthy businessman, sportsman and philanthropist, was awarded, for all sorts of reasons, the Grand Order of the Crown of Italy. Wanting to do something in return, in 1909 he commissioned a superb and very valuable football trophy to be competed for by various countries, the final to be played in Italy's Turin Stadium. The English Football Association was invited to enter a team but, without any good reason that anybody could see, declined the offer. Lipton nevertheless insisted that England had to be represented and it seems that one of his employees who had been a football referee in the north of England proposed that West Auckland would fit the bill.

"There are many today who'll think that this was a ludicrous suggestion; the team was made up mainly of miners, rank amateurs who'd never even done anything in the FA Amateur Cup while Bishop Auckland, just three miles away, had a proven track record. No matter; the West Auckland lads pawned all they had to travel to Italy and beat FC Winterhour 2-0 in the final. Remember that these were local miners matched against the cream of Europe's footballers!

"Two years later, in 1911 they were invited to return to Italy to defend their title as football's world champions, the first to hold that honour, and on that occasion they beat the mighty Juventus in a staggering 6-1 victory. According to the rules of the competition, West Auckland having won the trophy on two consecutive occasions, it was theirs to keep.

"They had to pawn it, however, to pay the costs of their second 'European holiday'. For £40 it went into the keeping of Mrs Lancaster, landlady of the local Wheatsheaf Pub until the club could redeem it for the same amount. Can you believe that this magnificent 32 inch high, solid silver statue was in her keeping until 1960 when it was bought back for £100? Incredible!

"In 1994, while on permanent display in West Auckland Workingmen's Club, the Sir Thomas Lipton Trophy was stolen and hasn't been seen since. Thank goodness a perfect copy's been made and can still be seen there today. So West Auckland AFC did, honestly, win the very first football World Cup and I think the time has long passed for that achievement to be officially recognised in the record books.

"And, by the way, somebody has to know who stole it and where it is today. I can't believe that anybody would melt it down just for the value of its silver content. There's still a reward of £2,000 for its safe return. So who's got it? Let's have it back – where it belongs."

John continued to work as a coach for the Football Association, assisted George Wardle, area coach for the F A, and also helped on the Full Badge course at Durham.

Crook Town was the next team to call on his playing services and he did well at the Foundry Fields ground but, after just one season, the famous Kingsway ground at Bishop Auckland beckoned and he was not about to refuse an invitation to play in the two blues strip of what has always been acknowledged as one of the world's greatest-ever amateur football clubs. This really was the stuff of which dreams are made and was where his playing career finally came to an end.

"I had a good run," John reflects. "I enjoyed myself and hope that I brought a bit of pleasure to those who paid to watch us play. The high point was when I was selected to play for Durham County against, and we beat, Yorkshire at Bishop Auckland's Kingsway ground. It was actually the day of Dad's funeral but my mother insisted that I played and I did so because I knew that he would have wanted me to.

"Walter Turnbull, one of the game's real gentlemen, asked me afterwards how much my expenses were. I hadn't worked them out but calculated that they were about ten shillings, 50 pence in today's money. He then took out a notebook and a bus timetable and told me that I was actually owed seven shillings and fourpence (37 pence) and he duly handed over precisely that amount; I had to smile!

"However, there was one thing which appalled me in my football career; as I gained more and more coaching qualifications it became increasingly obvious to me that we, the players, weren't being told how to play. We were simply being told to get out there and try hard. Tactics and working on individual players didn't come into the equation. At that time, there weren't enough Full Badge coaches even to go round the Football League and I still feel that, even now, the standard of coaching on offer isn't what it should be.

"Too many clubs, both professional and amateur, fail to send players on coaching courses early enough and as often as they should. Too many people are of the opinion that professional footballers don't need coaching but they do. They need to be told what to do and how to do it. That's why Terry Venables is so brilliant as a coach; he works on skills, building up moves and he goes on repeating this procedure. The players know that he's good and they're prepared to work for him and at his direction.

"This might sound a bit controversial but I think that when a player believes that he no longer needs coaching then he's not going to make any more progress up the football ladder. It's a mistake many have made and continue to make. Such people have grown 'too big for their boots'. Of course natural talent's a prerequisite for any great sportsman but such talent has to be brought on and coaching and experience are the only ways in which that can be achieved."

When Burton was chairman of recreation on Sedgefield Borough Council, he invited Venables, then at Barcelona, to send a youth team to compete in a tournament. Venables agreed, but no team ever arrived. The two men met some time later and John asked Terry what had gone wrong. Venables explained that there were some 200 teams with players from the age of five upwards closely connected with Barcelona FC and he just did not know which one to send because those not selected would have been offended.

"Barcelona has a 'sporting club' system which is universal almost across Europe," John explains, "but we've been slow to latch on to it. In a way, school football has hindered its introduction. That's not to damn the work going on in schools. It's terrific, but we need somehow to combine our school football set-up with the European club system.

"The Government has started to provide more funding to pay for coaches to go into schools and this has to lead to a better standard of coaching in the long term so it's not impossible, but we've got to get much more money into the grass roots of the game and we desperately need many more fully qualified coaches. Too much has been spent for too long on top dressing. I want to stress and to be perfectly clear that in no way am I knocking the efforts of PE teachers; I was one myself and I know that they do need to be experts at everything.

"We've also got to go along with the idea that boys and girls under the age of 11 or even 13 shouldn't be playing in teams of 11. That's not the way forward. In that system the children don't get enough possession of the ball; they don't have enough space and they certainly don't have the stamina for a 60-minute match. We need them to be playing six- or seven-a-side so that they can feel the ball, run, play to feet and have a sense of achievement at the end of the game."

Despite all of Burton's achievements in the game, he has one major regret. "Sadly, I was never in a position to play for Sunderland. It was what would now be called 'the impossible dream'. I was good but I was never that good.

"Nowadays the Sunderland chairman Bob Murray calls me every week or two for one reason or another and I always answer his call by advising him that I might not be available to play the following Saturday. 'Damn,' he says, 'never mind; I'll have to make do with the squad I've got.'

"If you want the truth, I'd give a fortune, mind you I haven't got one, just to run out onto the Stadium of Light as a player. Isn't it time that they inaugurated a veterans' team? Perhaps Tony might like to join me! Don't tell him I said that."

6: If music be the food of love

ALONGSIDE sport, politics and family life, music has always played an important part in the lives of John and Lily Burton. She plays the organ at church and the piano while he is more than proficient on the banjo and guitar.

Their musical tastes are wide-ranging and they have an extensive collection of records and CDs, started seriously during the rock 'n' roll era of the mid-1950s. They like almost everything from Elvis Presley through Lonnie Donegan, Woody Guthrie, Pete Seeger and other folk music, jazz, especially as played by Chris Barber, to Frank Sinatra, Ella Fitzgerald, church music and the classics.

"I think we've got a bit of everything," John muses, "but whatever happened to all of our 78s and 45s: Elvis Presley, Buddy Holly and the Crickets, Paul Anka, Connie Francis, Bobby Darin, the Platters and the rest? They'd be worth a bob or two today but, like our famous pedal bin, most of them just disappeared along the way. I suppose we gave some away and threw others out during our several house moves. We even made some of them into plantpots! I mean, how many people still have machines that play 78s? They tell me that even CDs are now old-fashioned.

"Like almost every youngster of our generation, Lily and I had a Dansette record player; it wasn't trendy to call it a gramophone and, anyway, it was electric but some of our friends still had those that you had to wind up. Like our old records, that Dansette just disappeared, probably to a jumble sale. Shame really."

He seriously knows his music. "Did you know that Donegan used to sing with Chris Barber's band in the early 1950s?" he asks. "We had Donnegan at Trimdon Labour Club just recently and he was still very good value for money."

The guitar which John used at the Parent Teacher Association concerts in Hoddesdon, in fact all through college too, was bought for him by his father and he taught himself to play.

"I just bought or borrowed a book of chords and picked up riffs and runs here and there," he says. "I wasn't really serious about it at first but, once I put my mind to it, I did get a lot better. I'd been forced as a child to go to hour-long piano lessons but I hated them. My first teacher was called Elsie Goodbody and she tried hard with me but I wanted to be out playing football with the other lads. Mind you, I must admit that the lessons gave me a useful grounding; I did learn to read music and I could play the piano tolerably well by the time I stopped going."

At college John played the guitar with others at parties and as a way of relaxing but he did not join any of the many groups at Bede who were more serious about their music and performing.

"It's funny that, isn't it?" muses Burton. "Both Tony (Blair) and I played guitar as teenagers but he saw it at the time as a route to fame and I didn't. Now I'm fractionally more famous as a singer than he is but he has a bigger following in other ways."

John never performed on stage at the folk club in Hoddesdon; he and Lily simply enjoyed a drink, soaked up the atmosphere and learned a number of songs from some of the greatest acts of the day. When they returned to the North-East, they continued to visit folk clubs. Lily and he started to practise singing together and popped into the Sun Inn at Stockton once or twice, enjoying performances by some of the region's folk stars. They began to visit the Castle Eden Folk Club in the Fir Tree and were soon singing there every week; they also appeared at The Bell in Horden where he met Bert Gelson, another former Wellfield scholar. That club was not doing particularly well at the time and Bert admitted to John that he had booked Tommy Gilfellon of The High Level Ranters and was worried about being able to pay him. Was there, asked Bert, anywhere in Trimdon Village which might attract an audience for folk music to help defray the costs?

"Well," John replied, "there's a perfect room at The Red Lion. I'll see the landlord and see what I can arrange for a Friday night. That's when people can pop out for a drink and a bit of entertainment and we'll not have too much pressure on us there to leave early! I'll advertise it around the village."

That first folk club at The Red Lion in the late 1960s was, to quote John, "absolutely heaving" and it went on that way for years. He and Lily regularly sang there together and guest artists also came along; a wonderful atmosphere soon developed and everybody knew that if they weren't there early they had no chance of a seat – in fact they were unlikely to get into the room.

John and Lily decided, after a short time, that it would be a sensible to get together a resident group so that if guest artists happened to be thin on the ground or if finances did not allow, quality entertainment would still be guaranteed. The group was originally known as The Trimdon Folk Band and they performed at the Red Lion for about eight years.

The original members were John, Lily, Dick Smith, Vincent English, a tin whistle player from Ryhope, plus "Eddie" – still to this day known to Burton only as "Eddie" – who played the spoons and sang the occasional song.

The line-up was short-lived and as John grew busier at school, the folk club's attendances started to decline and it was relocated to The Bird In Hand.

He, of course, continued to visit The Red Lion and met again Edwin and

Marshal Thomas, a successful singing duo in the 1960s. The Lion's landlady persuaded John to start singing there again and so, for a short time, there were two folk clubs operating in the village.

There was, John admits, "a bit of awkwardness between them". The Bird In Hand's club was more traditional than The Red Lion where artistes were not reprimanded if part of their performance was not strictly 'folk'. Soon The Red Lion gained the upper hand and was once more "heaving with people".

By now, John, Edwin and Marshal Thomas, Brian Stubbs, Gordon Dyke and Brian Childs were all part of the resident band. Wyn Morgan, a peripatetic music teacher like Gordon Dyke, joined for a while playing his double bass; today he farms in Wales but still performs with them whenever able. Colin Thompson was also involved.

As the band grew bigger and were no longer confined to Trimdon, a new name was required. John suggested that of the local river, the Skerne which rose in Trimdon Village at the bottom of the Watchbank, and it stuck. Many thought Skerne was a strange name for a folk group but when the Bank of England issued a £5 note in the early-1990s with George Stephenson's famous Locomotion No 1 crossing the bridge over the River Skerne in Darlington, the band suddenly found themselves passing through the hands of the whole country.

When Peter Brookes moved into the village in the early-1980s, Skerne had as many as 12 musicians on stage – if everyone turned up. In fact, the band's first album was called Better Late Than Never, since they had a reputation for not being on time for their appearances.

"Audiences didn't mind that," John recalls, "as long as we got there in the end. We all had such different jobs that getting together in one place at any specified time was never easy. Sometimes we'd start a set with whoever was there and then we'd be gradually joined on stage by the latecomers. It was par for the course and audiences accepted that and do so even today. It's simply the way it has to be! We don't do it for a living and, if one of us can't make an appearance, the rest just cope."

Today, John does not have a copy of Better Late Than Never. "The ones I did have were all given away to friends or as raffle prizes; but I'm still proud of it, as we all are," he says.

Skerne played, and still play, at lots of charity functions and their current repertoire is what John describes as "popular folk". Northern songs, Irish ones and some popularised by The Spinners and The Dubliners are all there; Ralph McTell's Streets of London is still heavily requested but Johnny Handle's The Collier Lad continues to be the most popular of all.

John Burton: The Grit in the Oyster

Skerne also appeared with Harry Secombe on the Highway television programme from Ushaw College, just outside Durham City, when The Collier Lad, along with two or three other Durham mining songs, was again featured.

The International Exchange Officer for County Durham then asked the group if they would like to travel to Rheinhausen in Germany as part of an exchange visit he was organising. They agreed to go and wherever Skerne performed, the German audiences loved their music and, since most of them spoke English well, language was not a barrier.

The group have since travelled to Tubingen in the south of Germany where a 20-year-old twinning arrangement still continues. "We'd arranged to meet Wyn at Dover docks and said he couldn't miss us because we were in a Scarlet Band Bus," recalls Burton. "But when we got there, there was no sign of him, so we had no alternative but to leave him to find his own way and get on the ferry.

"When we got on board, there he was. 'Where've you been?' I asked. 'I got on the wrong bus,' he said. It turned out that there was another Scarlet Band Bus going to Dover that day.

"But then I said: 'How did you get on the wrong bus when you're carrying your double bass? What sort of driver stops for a complete stranger carrying a double bass and lets him on the bus?'."

Skerne have also travelled to what was then the USSR to play in Kostromo, "a lovely old city". The group played in schools, technical colleges, ambulance stations, works canteens and other venues that they couldn't work out the purpose of, but they were always well-received. The Russians had never before experienced musicians and songs such as these.

"It still makes me smile a bit wryly," remembers John, "to think that not only did we have to contribute significantly from our own pockets, and we didn't have much money ourselves, to be part of that tour but we also had to perform for free! We did get a small grant from the county for being a 'youth group'; well, we were all in our 30s and 40s, the oldest 'youth group' ever, I suppose, and the Russians simply had no money to pay us.

"They treated us as if we were beings who'd just landed from Mars; they'd never come across anything like us. We even had to sign autographs! Still, it was a fantastic experience and worth every kopek, or pound, we didn't receive. The hospitality was tremendous.

"One of the funniest things was that the Russians had been expecting a group of teenagers, and no way did we fit into that category, but, when they realised that there'd been some sort of breakdown in communication, out came the vodka and that broke down all barriers."

Skerne also went on to perform in Slovakia and John continues to correspond with people he met there.

The group recorded a couple of tracks for the Full Head of Steam CD produced in part to mark the 175th anniversary of the opening, in 1825, of the Stockton and Darlington Railway.

Skerne's current line-up, when the whole group manages to get together roughly on time, includes Burton, banjo and vocals, Edwin Thomas on guitar and vocals, Marshal Thomas, harmonica and vocals, Peter Brookes on guitar with vocals, Brian Priestley on accordian and vocals, Wyn Morgan on double bass and Dermott Roddy on violin.

John used to play only the guitar but, when The Trimdon Folk Band started, he bought and learned to play the banjo to create a different sound.

"All we need now to have a Top 10 hit," John jokes, "is for the Prime Minister to join us on guitar and lead vocals. Now that would be a first, wouldn't it, but, somehow, I can't see it happening in the near future. Perhaps we should all grow our hair, wear skintight white trousers, travel around in an old Ford van and change our name to something like Ugly Rumours!"

7: To stir without great argument

JOHN Burton is best known for his political career and yet he did not venture into that arena until he was in his mid-twenties.

It was 1966, his father had just died and John and Lily were living in Trimdon Village. His parents had been lifelong Labour supporters and workers and John had always been aware of their views.

"I suppose it was wanting to take a full part in what went on in the village, a genuine belief that everybody should make some sort of contribution to the life of their community, that made me take over Dad's role as Secretary to the Parochial Church Council," he says. "Lily and I loved the old church (St Mary Magdalene, we knew the people who worshipped there and I just really wanted to carry on Dad's work.

"Mind you, I wasn't completely sure that I was up to the job but I'd watched him do it over the years, I could take minutes and could speak pretty coherently so I gave it a go. I think I was a bit nervous at first, frightened of saying the wrong thing at the wrong time but those jitters soon disappeared and the rest of the team were very supportive.

"Whenever I see The Vicar of Dibley on television, I think of those days but I must point out that we were never as bad as that lot, although there are elements of reality in the programme. There were certainly plenty of humorous moments in our meetings but I was never such a pedantic secretary as the guy in the series."

John's religious beliefs also extended into life outside the Church. His political thinking was inextricably linked to his Christianity.

"I suppose I'm most accurately described as a Christian Socialist and I think that's what Tony (Blair) is too. Our views, our opinions and our outlooks have always been remarkably similar. That's one of the reasons we've always got on so well."

In 1966, John joined Trimdon Village Labour Party which, at that time, had only about a dozen members.

"The chairman was George Terrans, well known throughout the county and almost everybody knew him as 'Mick' but I always called him George. He was an incredibly powerful man, involved with the National Union of Mineworkers. From the district council he moved on to the County Council. He became leader of the Labour Group on it, then had two years as vice-chairman and two more as its chairman.

"It's funny, you know, but he was never a driver and used public transport to get to the remotest places. He must have spent thousands of hours on buses and trains and yet he was never known to be late for a meeting."

George Terrans, who had been a friend of Donald Burton for years, persuaded John to take a vacant seat on the parish council.

"By then, in the late 1960s, I had much more confidence," says Burton. "I could project my voice well, the length of a football pitch when necessary, knew when to keep quiet and when to speak up and spoke slowly and articulately at meetings. I think that the other members were pleased to see a 'younger' person on the council.

"There are still those who continue to regard the work of parish councils as mundane and trivial but it's not, far from it, and it does have its lighter moments. There's one I remember particularly well and it really is a true story although it's more like something from a situation comedy writer's pen. The parish council really did change things for the good and local people watched it happen. In the course of time I was elected Chairman of the Policy and Resources Committee and one of my first jobs was to oversee discussions on whether Trimdon Village Parish Council should, or should not, appoint a full-time, salaried parish clerk. Now, this would turn out to be an important and, locally, historic decision and the debate was frequently fairly heated.

"We were running all sorts of schemes to improve the village and there was a real need for somebody to co-ordinate them all. When I thought that the matter had been fully discussed I called for a vote. Three were for the appointment of the full-time clerk and three were against so from the chair I used my casting vote in favour of it.

"That was the day I found out what it meant in politics to stand up for what you believe to be right and it wasn't long before our decision was proved to have been the right one. Things started to happen; we took on some trainees to repair roads and footpaths; the local vicar borrowed a steamroller, and drove it, to compress the tarmac. Raymond Ayre agreed to supervise, free of charge, the installation of floodlights round the church if all the gear was provided, which it was. The trainees had by then been awarded the title 'F Troop' and they really worked their socks off. Everybody remembers them."

One of the most difficult meetings John had to chair concerned the request by the parish clerk Peter Tate for a telephone to be installed, at the parish council's expense, in the sexton's house. The sexton looked after the cemetery, Peter argued, and people often needed to get in touch with him urgently.

"There are people who want to reserve plots," Peter went on, "undertakers who want to have graves dug – and others who need to arrange monumental erections."

John Burton: The Grit in the Oyster

After the briefest of silences, during which Peter and the rest realised what he had just said, John leapt to his feet and moved that the required telephone should be installed immediately and that all those present be given the number at once!

John's friend Terry Ward became a member of the new Sedgefield District Council in 1973 and, in 1976, suggested that John should stand for election to it too. While John was elected, Terry lost his seat, and so, although he knew a few councillors well, he attended his first Labour Group Meeting of the council alone. Recognising that he was a novice in an unfamiliar situation, he went, sat and listened. He was amazed by what he heard.

The first speaker stood up and made a speech which lasted for about three minutes. When he sat down, another councillor answered him. Both had been councillors for a very long time. John did not understand one word said by either of them; their arguments were mumbled, garbled, incoherent and made no sense at all.

He was told after the meeting that it was always like that. In 1976, dinosaurs still roamed the Labour Party; they'd been elected so long ago they had forgotten why they were there, and the ordinary man in the street was so disenchanted with the lot of them, he didn't bother to stand against them. And so the dinosaurs still ruled the earth.

Some elder statesmen, like George Terrans, did, however, contribute significantly to local politics and were more than happy to see younger people entering the political arena just as long as they understood from the outset that they were there to serve others and not just to further their own ambition.

But unless young councillors worked for very understanding employers, they mostly soon fell by the wayside. They could not afford to take unpaid leave to attend council meetings during working hours. Local authority and trade union employees, along with those who worked for some of the nationalised industries, were usually able to arrange paid absence for the necessary 48 half-days each year but they did so at the cost of promotion. Burton's headteacher told him, kindly but bluntly, that he needed to decide whether to aim for his own headship or to pursue his political aims. John chose the latter course and continues to wonder whether that decision also somehow involved fateful intervention.

Because councils were such a closed club, the wider world was left outside their doors. The Labour Party itself did not help. In fact, Burton remembers with bitterness how, in the mid-1970s, the party went out of its way to slam the door in the face of the wider world.

Burton recalls meeting a Transport and General Workers' Union member as late as 1984 in Stockton. "He explained that he'd been an active trade union member all his working life. He wasn't from the Trimdon area but he told me he'd made several attempts to join his local Labour Party and, each time, he'd been told that it was full," says Burton. "I told him that this couldn't possibly be true, that it was impossible for a branch to be 'full' and that they weren't allowed to say that. Those who were in charge simply couldn't be processing the membership applications or were keeping new people out just to maintain the status quo. They obviously didn't want the cosy power they had to be wrested from their grasp by whatever means and were making all sorts of excuses to retain it, come Hell or high water. There really were some Labour Party branches which had just four or five members and that suited them very nicely, thank you.

"It was democracy in one way, I suppose," Burton reasons, "but it wasn't right. Local people weren't properly involved. They didn't feel that they had a say."

And so people turned their backs on Labour. "People didn't want this party which held endless meetings where nothing constructive was ever mooted or done; where everything was destructive," says Burton.

"Nobody was coming up with any really bright ideas to move things forward. It was always 'you can't do this, you can't do that, you mustn't do this, you shouldn't do that' and so on – and on and on! The Constituency Labour Party was getting nowhere at all."

And the Sedgefield party was not unusual. "After its 1983 election debacle, the Labour Party nationally just lost its way completely," Burton says, "and the far left Militant and the like saw their opportunity to take over.

"The majority of their support was in the big towns and cities. The whole situation was a mess, a real mess. Some of the real left-wingers were out to destroy the Labour Party and, let's call a spade a spade, there was a degree of corruption. There were people in the party at that time who were members simply to get what they could, by whatever means, out of the party; they weren't terribly interested in the Labour Party and they couldn't care less what happened to the country. They were out for themselves.

"Many of them were just power freaks who wanted to climb as high as they could and feather their own nests along the way. This was going on in other political parties, too, and it reached a point where politics stopped being important. As far as Labour was concerned, and I mean nationwide, too many local politicians ceased to be interested in the well-being and future of the party nationally.

"Those days had to come to an abrupt end. I knew that things needed to change, and was determined to do it, but I had to stay on the inside to bring it about."

Trimdon Village Labour Party was the first to feel the wind of change.

John Burton: The Grit in the Oyster

He says: "There was a national Labour Party rule which said that prospective members had also to be in a trade union. I didn't think that was fair and there was what can best be described as a storm over how I dealt with it. There are some people who were, to put it in the northern vernacular, 'gobsmacked' and who would still say that it was even tantamount to Armageddon, the ultimate struggle if you like, but I went ahead anyway, removing the knives from my back as I did so.

"Eventually, however, they started to stab me in the front so that made things a bit easier. I lost a few 'acquaintances' (they called themselves 'friends'), in the process but that didn't worry me one jot. I knew that I was going against the rules, but also I knew, I knew in my heart, just knew, somehow, where the local party needed to be and that there was only one way that it could possibly ever get there.

"In our party in Trimdon, we started to let in anybody who wanted to join, trade union members or not – and there were, it has to be said, many more than we thought."

Mel Foster, the owner of the garage at the top of the village, and his wife were invited to join. Foster agreed with one proviso: he had been a member of a trade union all of his working life until he had bought his own business and had reached the point where he could no longer see any personal value in union membership. He had always been a stalwart supporter of the Labour Party and was more than happy to make significant financial contributions to it but he could not join a trade union just so that he could become a fully-fledged party member. He even offered to write a cheque for £100 to the party on the spot just to join, but refused to demonstrate his support by becoming a trade union member.

Burton mulled it over, and then signed him up.

Burton also allowed in people who could not afford to pay the full subscription of £15 to £18. As long they were prepared to make some contribution, no matter how little, weekly, monthly or annually, they were acceptable.

"We talked to people who were fervent supporters of Labour, whose parents and grandparents had also been of the same mind, but who really were having the most enormous difficulty in making ends meet and putting bread on the family table, let alone worrying about paying membership fees to the party," says Burton. "From those who wanted to join we got an average of £5 per person. We took leaflets to every one of the 1,300 households in Trimdon Village and said we'd be back within the next three or four days.

"We started in Meadow Road and three weeks later we were still in Meadow

Road because someone in about every third house joined. Having covered three streets, we ended up with two hundred new members and even now, some 15 years later, we still haven't finished in the village. We did go off and do the same in other areas of the constituency so that slowed down our work in Trimdon."

The local TGWU, which was also looking for change, supported the moves of the Trimdon party, and Burton led many discussions in the mid-1980s, sometimes with Blair present, based on the hypothesis that if people were allowed to join the Labour Party without needing first to be in a trade union then they might ultimately decide to join a union too. That was, it seems, precisely what happened in many cases; today, for example, the local branch of the TGWU is one of the biggest in the north of England.

But in the constituency, as nationally, there was opposition. Burton feels it came from the extreme left of the party which called itself the Trades' Council. "They complained bitterly and loudly that we were allowing in people who were completely ineligible for membership and their complaining was extremely vociferous," recalls Burton.

But Burton and his cohorts weathered the storm. At times, it felt as if it would have been easier to walk away. But to Burton, this was nothing less than a Christian Socialist crusade, a quest to see justice done.

"In the end," Burton says, "we delivered what people wanted. At the end of the day, it was nothing more than common sense.

"We'd listened to what local people wanted from the Labour Party and we did something about it – but to do it we had to break the rules," admits Burton. "We had no qualms about doing so, none at all. You might reason that if people don't like the flavour ice cream you're trying to sell then you either stop or you change the flavours. We changed the flavours."

A 'new' Labour Party was evolving.

It had to, if only to shadow the community from which it traditionally drew its support. Since 1946, John had heard some of the country's greatest political orators – and some who were not of such a high standard – at the annual Durham Miners' Gala, locally known as Durham Big Meeting.

From its inception in 1871, it was one of the most important socialist events on the northern calendar. Since the closures of the mines in the 1980s, its importance has slipped, especially from its heyday in the 1930s and 1940s when more than 200,000 people were attracted to Durham City – shop windows had to be planked up, not to thwart rioters, but to prevent individuals falling through the plate glass as the mass of humanity swept around the narrow, twisty streets.

The miners and their families came with their bands from all over the North-East and beyond, and they processed and danced in a huge, snaking throng behind their colliery banners and bandsmen, making their way across Elvet Bridge, past the Royal County Hotel, where political and mining worthies waved to them from the balcony, then along Old Elvet and on to the racecourse by the riverside. John would himself one day have the privilege of standing on that famous balcony – the first occasion was when he was honoured for travelling with Skerne to Germany where the group raised £18,000 to support the miners' strike of 1984.

But the Gala was not just a huge picnic where miners and their families came to eat and drink and be merry. They also came to demonstrate their solidarity as a fraternity with one another, and with the Labour Party.

John remembers that on his first visit his family walked behind the Trimdon Grange banner and his father explained to him that those banners draped with black crepe were from collieries where one or more miners had lost their lives during the previous year.

As a child, John played with the other children but, as the years passed, gradually the political speeches from the platforms started to mean more to him.

As an adult, he once dressed up in bowler hat and tailcoat and danced, complete with umbrella, at the front of a New Orleans style jazz band – two pints of beer in Hesleden Workingmen's Club at 7.30am gave him the courage.

"When we were right in front of the Royal County Hotel balcony, we stopped and the band played the most wonderful jazz/gospel version of Just A Closer Walk With Thee. It was different and it went down a storm. Neil Kinnock was on the balcony that day and you could see from his face that he really enjoyed it."

But as the 1970s played out, the mood of the Big Meeting began to change. "It degenerated over a number of years, long before all the pits were gone, into an opportunity for almost anyone who wanted to do so to have a go, in public, at the Labour leadership," says Burton. "Suddenly the likes of Neil Kinnock could do nothing right; it was their fault, claimed the ranters, that the pits were being closed, it was their fault that Labour wasn't in government, in fact it was even their fault that it was raining!

"And people like Kinnock had to sit there and listen to these people. It really wasn't a fair way to treat anybody. They showed not just a lack of respect but something that was near to, if not actually, contempt.

"Eventually, the day came when Neil refused to attend any more Galas at Durham and after that both John Smith and Tony have followed his example. It's a great shame but enough was enough. Nobody should have had to sit through the kind of unmitigated verbal tongue-lashing that was being dished out by some speakers. Even the audience was frequently embarrassed. Neil sat on the platform for the last time in 1989 and I applauded his decision not to go back. He was right not to do so."

Even in the North-East today, it is a statement that will not be universally popular, but throughout his political career Burton has always been true to himself and spoken up at what he considered to be the right time for what he believed to be the right cause.

He made mistakes but learned his trade in a hard school, and was someone to be reckoned with in the local Labour Party. In 1988-89 he was Chairman of Sedgefield District Council.

He made political friends and political enemies. He also made waves, and there were those who did not enjoy getting wet.

8: A sympathy in choice

ON MONDAY, May 9, 1983, Conservative Prime Minister Margaret Thatcher called a General Election for June 9.

Although John Burton did not know it at the time, fate was about to intervene again in his life and to play him a card which would partner him politically with Tony Blair. In the unlikely setting of Trimdon Village, there was to be an extraordinary meeting which would change British politics and the lives of both men forever.

Blair, a barrister living in Hackney who had just turned 30, had been searching for a seat for three years. In 1980, had had tried for Middlesbrough; in 1981, he had tried for Teesside Thornaby (now Stockton South). In 1982, he had been selected for the Beaconsfield by-election, but had come a poor third in a safe Conservative seat at the height of the Falklands War.

By 1983, with the election called, his time was running out. His wife Cherie had already found a seat – albeit an unwinnable one in Kent – and the two of them had an understanding that when one of them made it to the House of Commons the other would sacrifice their political ambitions to look after the family. But then he heard that the newly-created constituency of Sedgefield in County Durham was the only one in the country yet to choose a Labour candidate.

"With it being a new constituency," Burton recalls, "made up of bits of others, the Labour group had taken its time sorting out its revamped internal organisation and selecting a candidate."

It was a part of the country with which Blair was quite familiar: in 1958 when he was five, his family had moved to nearby Durham City where he had attended the Chorister School until 1966.

Blair was staying with a friend just outside Durham City in the village of Shincliffe, where his family had lived in the mid-1960s, and was attempting to find out which Labour branches in Sedgefield had still not submitted a nomination. He had contacted George Ferguson, the secretary of the Sedgefield Constituency Labour Party, to obtain the names and addresses of all the branch secretaries. The Trimdon Village branch, he noticed, was one of those which had yet to nominate or even endorse a candidate. So, on Tuesday, May 10, he tried to phone the branch secretary – one John Burton.

But every time Blair dialled he heard the 'number unobtainable' tone. After several attempts, and, just as he was about to give up, it occurred to him that he might be using the wrong area code. He was. Instead of prefixing 0740, then widespread across much of Sedgefield, he actually needed 0429, the code for Trimdon Village. He decided to try one last time. If he did not get through then, he told himself, he was going home. Sedgefield, obviously, was not meant for him.

Suddenly, Blair heard the ringing tone. "It was like music," he remembers. "It was just the noise of a telephone making its usual connection but it was not what I had been getting earlier and it sounded great. All I needed then was for someone friendly to pick it up."

Blair had timed his call so that although it was early in the morning, it was no so early that it would get someone out of bed, and not so late that this John Burton fellow would have left for work.

Burton, in fact, was just on his way out to school in Sedgefield. He was in a hurry and could have done without being held up by an unsolicited call from an unknown person.

"The caller said to me that he had noticed that Trimdon Village Labour Party hadn't nominated anyone yet and wondered whether he could talk to me about becoming our nominee," says Burton. Burton was not really all that interested in the forthcoming General Election as he was far from happy with the Labour Party's stance nationally. In any case, he and his team had enough to keep themselves busy in their own patch as he and Terry Ward had just been re-elected to Sedgefield District Council.

"I was determined to push for better recreational facilities for everybody in the area," says Burton. "That was my priority. We were constantly, or so it seems in retrospect, having meetings and discussions about local politics and the one topic which kept on intruding, like a boil needing to be lanced, was the matter of what was wrong with the Labour Party nationally at that time."

But, he says, there was "just a something" in the caller's voice which caused him to listen and to give a considered answer.

"Look," he said to Blair, "I'm just on my way out to work but a few of us have arranged a sort of celebratory meeting tomorrow evening. Why don't you come and join us then and we'll listen to what you have to say? Let's say about eight o'clock. Alright? Look forward to meeting you."

The arrangement made, Burton put down the telephone and hurried off to work. For Blair, who had been hoping for a meeting that day, it meant more hanging around as the election drew closer and closer. The following morning, he was about to call Burton to politely decline the invitation so he could return to London. Something, however, stopped him from doing so.

"I don't know what it was," Blair admits. "I can't tell you. Really, I can't. I was missing Cherie like mad and just wanted to go home – but there was something in that guy's voice which insisted that I had to meet him and his colleagues. I just had to be there and, so, I was. Whatever, as it transpired, I borrowed a car, put on a good grey suit, my best, got lost three or four times on the way – well, there are a lot of Trimdons, the Colliery, the Village and the Station, none of them well signposted at the time – and I arrived, eventually, at 9 Front Street South, Trimdon Village."

He was about an hour late. But again he hesitated. He almost did not get out of the car.

"The house looked really nice but I did wonder what I was letting myself in for," says Blair. "Who was this fellow John Burton? Why the celebration? Why should I be included in it and why should he and his friends be remotely interested in supporting the political aspirations of a young barrister from London? I had no idea. I would find the answers to these questions only if I knocked – so I did.

"A man with a shock of greying hair, a moustache and smiling eyes opened the door. Shaking my hand, he invited me inside. This was my first unforgettable meeting with John Burton."

This first meeting between the two men has practically become the stuff of legends. According to that legend, the crowd inside the house was not discussing the forthcoming General Election nor even analysing the just-past local election. They were watching football on the television, the European Cup Winners' Cup Final between Real Madrid and Aberdeen.

"A story has gone round that I opened the door to Tony, invited him in and told him to sit down, have a beer and keep quiet until the end of the game – which went to extra time – or he wouldn't have a hope of gaining the nomination from Trimdon Village," says Burton. "Believe me – I never said any such thing!"

The match was on in the house, and many present did have at least one eye on it, but they were there primarily to write a thank-you leaflet to all who had supported them in the recent district and parish council elections.

Present with John and Lily Burton were social worker Peter Brookes who was also a member of Burton's Skerne band; the branch's youth officer Simon Hoban; Paul Trippett, who worked for Sedgefield council, and Terry Ward, the newly-elected councillor and health service union activist.

Blair was invited to help himself to a can of beer or a glass of wine and to watch the football while the leaflet was finished. But as the drama of the match unfolded, and extra time loomed, the one-eyes became two-eyes, and soon everyone was engrossed – including Blair. However, Burton noticed that the outsider was also weighing up those around him and the situation in which he found himself.

Eventually Aberdeen scored the winner, the television was switched off, the leaflet was completed, and the questioning began. What was his policy on the nuclear deterrent, on health, what were his feelings about Europe, what did he think about the state of the Labour Party...

Burton believes that Blair was surprised at the speed with which his questioners had switched from football to politics. He answered well but did not try to ingratiate himself with them. As Burton says, he was extremely honest about where he stood and he certainly did not give the answers they had expected, something which came as a surprise.

"We gave him a good grilling and although he was astute enough to have told us what he thought we wanted to hear, he didn't," says Burton. "That's what gradually swung us from initial apathy to a sort of subdued enthusiasm. There was something engaging about his personality. He had a presence about him, charisma I suppose you'd call it. He wanted to get into Parliament to make a difference to society. That was why I'd got involved in politics and that was one of the reasons, possibly the main one, although I didn't say so straight away, that I felt we should support him."

As the questioning came to an end very late in the evening, Trippett took Burton into the back room and explained that, before he had known that Blair was to be present, he had intended to suggest that Burton should be the nominee from the Trimdon Village branch. Before going any further and saying anything to Blair, Trippett urged, Burton should decide whether he was prepared to stand.

Burton had already considered this possibility, but had kept his thoughts to himself. After the briefest of pauses, he answered Trippett: "Look, we've got this young chap. He's obviously very clever. I think there's something special about him and it'll be easier for me to get him selected than for you to do the same for me. You know that you're never a prophet in your own land. I know that I'm a good district councillor but to the people who matter in this thing I'll still be seen as just a good district councillor. Thanks for the thought but I think we should give Blair our support."

Trippett agreed and the two of them returned to the room. After a few minutes during which he spoke with the others, Burton told Blair that they would support him.

"The one thing you need to understand," he warned the nominee, "is that we're really going to try hard to get you in."

Burton knew just how difficult a job it would be. "On the cards," he says, "this young man didn't have the remotest cat in hell's chance of becoming the prospective Labour candidate for the Sedgefield constituency. Everything, and I mean everything, was stacked against him. On paper, he couldn't possibly succeed; he was on a hiding to nothing, he really was, and he knew it, but he and we were prepared to give it a lot more than our best shot. We believed in him and, just as importantly, he trusted us with his future. Mind you, our credibility was on the line too. We'd said: 'Look, here's a bloke; he's different, he's young, he's intelligent, he's charismatic, he's talking the language that we're talking; like us he knows that the Labour Party's got to change; it's lost touch with the people, it's got to be bigger, it has to learn to communicate'.

"Those were the reasons why we decided to push him – and to push him for all that he and we were worth. The Labour Party locally was being dominated by one or two left-wing people but there were those who were prepared to admit that things had to change, people who were ready to stand up and be counted, who were no longer prepared to sit and, out of fear, say nothing. What we tried to do was to open meetings, to get people to come to them. In Trimdon Village even today we're still breaking the rules. Anybody who wants to can come to Labour Party meetings and they don't have to be a party member; maybe one day they'll decide to join. If they do, that's great but if they don't – well, so what?"

Before Blair left Burton's house that evening, the wheels were already in motion trying to engineer his selection. There were just nine days in which to achieve a miracle. The Labour Party candidate for the Sedgefield constituency would be selected in Spennymoor Town Hall on Friday, May 20 but if Blair's name was to go before that meeting, a number of other deadlines had to be met and an array of obstacles had to be overcome.

Trippett decided to take a fortnight's holiday to show Blair the patch since he knew where the people who mattered lived; Brookes loaned Blair his car, and Burton got the names of the delegates who would be at the selection meeting so that they could go round and talk to them all.

Ward decided not to be involved. He liked Blair but did not feel at the time that he could support him. Phil Wilson, though, took his place. Wilson had worked for Burton and Ward's re-election to the district council but had been away at a Civil and Public Servants Association conference on the night Blair appeared on the scene.

"When I got back on the Saturday, Paul Trippett said I had to support this bloke Blair," says Wilson. "When I met him that weekend, I too was taken by him.

"John Burton said I had to ignore his posh accent, because he was Cabinet material. He wasn't from our sort of background but he could get on with anyone."

As for Blair himself, he readily took up John and Lily's invitation to move into 9, Front Street South with them and their children and he was soon one of the family. As Lily says, he just fitted in.

"The children took turns to sleep on the floor in what became 'their' room because we had only three bedrooms but we managed," she says. "To them it was not an inconvenience, just a big adventure."

"There wasn't any point in him staying anywhere else," says her husband. "Time was so tight that we had to have him at the centre of things all the time, to be there precisely when he was needed. His stay actually lasted, on and off, for 18 months until they bought Myrobella. Cherie often stayed there too."

The clock continued to tick relentlessly and the Blair campaign, planned in the most intricate and minute detail, gathered momentum. With Wilson joining Burton, Brookes and Trippett on the Blair bandwagon, the group soon acquired a number of titles such as The Trimdon Posse, The Famous Five and, less well-known, Blair's Backing Group. With hindsight, this last was the most appropriate since some of them were involved with music and they were about to have a hit, albeit of a political nature!

The dining room of 9, Front Street South was turned into something like a wartime command centre. Lily Burton, an essential element of the campaign and always an excellent sounding board, recalls: "All we needed to complete the picture was a huge table in the middle of the room with WRAF girls wearing headsets pushing pieces of wood around it to show the positions of our friends and 'bandits'. Every empty piece of wall was soon covered with maps, lists, photographs, schedules, reminder notes and pen portraits of everybody who was, in any way, somebody in the constituency. It looked like chaos but it was highly organised. Sometimes there'd be three or four conversations going on at the same time and people had to try to make sense of them."

Burton, the only one of "The Famous Five" to have a vote on May 20, knew that most who would attend the selection meeting were already committed. But his line of attack was to look further ahead, beyond the first ballot at that gathering, to enlist support for Blair in any subsequent votes.

"But the first thing we had to do," Burton smiles, "was to actually get him a nomination. Without a nomination, you can't be shortlisted and the nomination was to be from our branch, Trimdon Village Labour Party. I was secretary of the branch. George Terrans, who was leader of Durham County Council, was the chairman. He was also chairman of the Constituency Labour Party (CLP). His skills in the chair are as legendary as he was. There wasn't anyone who could put one over on George. As they say today, he'd been there, done that, got the T-shirt – in fact, he had a wardrobe full of them. To those who were prepared to watch and listen he was an excellent political tutor. I certainly learned a lot from him."

Burton telephoned Terrans and explained that he and some others were in favour of giving the branch nomination to this young chap called Blair. Could a special branch meeting be convened on the morning of Saturday, May 14? Terrans could see no problem and said he would inform the CLP secretary who would arrange for the meeting to be held at Trimdon Village Community College, and for the members to be told.

"On that Saturday morning, Tony arrived and so did several other hopefuls including Hilary Armstrong, Frank Robson, David Taylor Gooby and, of course, the favourite Les Huckfield," says Burton. "All of them wanted our nomination because the more they had the more impressive they looked; all wanted to proffer a sort of bulging political portfolio. It was agreed that each prospective nominee would be allowed to speak for five minutes and could then answer questions, the same ones to each candidate, for a further five.

"They spoke in alphabetical order so Tony followed Hilary who opened the proceedings. He maintains to this day that his offering was the worst speech he has ever made but I didn't think it was at all bad. He was certainly, and by his own admission, extremely nervous – which didn't help him – but you have to remember that Sedgefield Constituency Labour Party was the last in the country to choose a candidate. That was a heavy burden to be carrying. If he blew his chance here, he had nowhere else to turn. It would all have been over for him."

Eventually, every speaker had been given the opportunity to put her or his case. It was decision time and there should then have been an exhaustive ballot; if, on the first vote, a candidate had received more than 50 per cent of the votes, the nomination would have been theirs. If not, then in each successive round the candidate who had received the lowest number of votes would drop out.

Burton, however, played the wildest of wild cards to abridge the proceedings.

Speaking directly to Terrans, he proposed: "Mr Chairman, in view of the fact that Tony Blair hasn't yet got a nomination, I move that we select him."

Terrans looked at Burton and asked if this motion was seconded. Trippett raised his hand. Terrans then put it to the meeting that the motion was a simple vote either for or against Blair. Both Terrans and Burton knew they were seriously bending the rules, but the meeting went with them, voting by 12 to four in favour of Blair.

But to salve their consciences, both were convinced that even if the rules had been adhered to rigidly and an exhaustive ballot held, Blair would still have won.

The next day, a Sunday, Burton drove to nearby Spennymoor to declare, in

*Top: John Burton meets his musical hero, Lonnie Donegan, in 2000. **Bottom left:** Burton hoping to promote squash at Trimdon County School. **Bottom right:** When Burton's daughter Caroline married Brian MacDonald in 1996, Blair was a guest. **Next page:** Burton giving the bride away*

Top: *The Famous Five: John Burton with (left to right) Peter Brookes, Terry Ward, Paul Trippett and Phil Wilson.* **Above:** *Burton and Wilson outside Trimdon Labour Club.* **Centre right:** *Brookes and Trippett.* **Right:** *Burton's son Jonathan and grandson Rikki-Lee*

*In place of the Sedgefield MP who is away on Prime Ministerial duties, John Burton receives a local Unison delegation protesting about the level of the minimum wage **(top)** and a Teesside group of protestors about disability issues **(bottom)**. Both are the gates of Myrobella in Trimdon in 1998*

Top: *John Burton, and pipe, during the 2001 General Election. Centre: Burton meeting Director of Communications Alastair Campbell (left) and Deputy Prime Minister John Prescott.* ***Left:*** *Burton receiving his first e-mail from the Prime Minister's website in 1999*

111

Top: *John and Lily Burton meet former US President Bill Clinton at the Labour Party Conference in Blackpool in 2002.* ***Bottom:*** *Watching with Blair as the 2001 election results come in*

Top: *John Burton and his wife Lily at home in Trimdon Village.* ***Bottom:*** *Burton with his banjo, outside St Mary Magdalene Church on Trimdon Village Green*

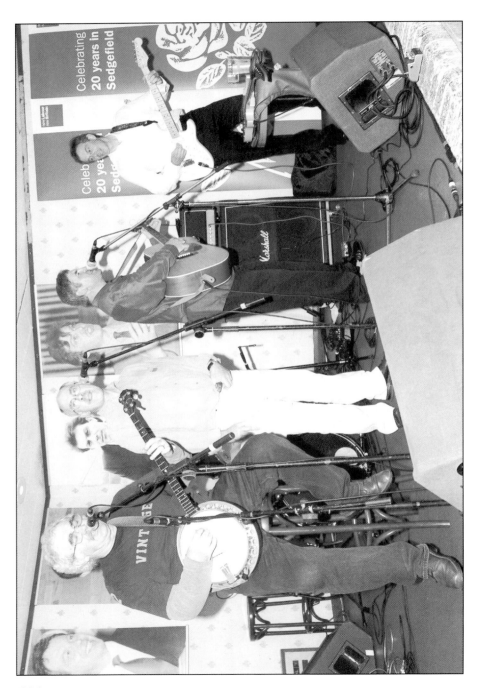

Facing page:
the Sedgefield
Supergroup
celebrating the
20th
anniversary of
Tony Blair's
election (left
to right): John
Burton,
David Hill,
Peter Brookes,
Blair.
Picture
courtesy of
Keith Taylor

Left: John
Burton and
his banjo at
the
anniversary
party in
2003.
Picture:
Stuart
Boulton

Over: Burton,
beer, sorted.
Picture: Keith
Taylor

115

SEDGEFIELD CONSTITUENCY LABOUR PARTY

Prospective Parliamentary Candidates   1983.

NAME	ADDRESS	AGE	NOMINATION
Armstrong H. J.	SUNDERLAND	37	A.S.T.M.S.
Barnett J.	MANCHESTER	59	E.E.T.P.U.
" "	" "	"	Chilton Lane LP
Blair A. C. L.	LONDON	30	Trimdon Village LP.
" " "	" "	"	T & G.W.U.
Giffin W.	YARM	49	Fire/B.U.
" " "	" "	"	Deaf Hill LP.
" " "	" "	"	Fishburn LP.
" " "	" "	"	Thornley LP.
Hepworth C. E.	DURHAM	40	G.M.B.A.T.U. (Matsa)
Huckfield L. J.	COVENTRY	41	N.U.M. Fishburn
" " "	" "	"	Deaf Hill LP.
" " "	" "	"	Wheatley Hill LP.
" " "	" "	"	Hutton Henry / Station Tn
" " "	" "	"	C.O.H.S.E.
" " "	" "	"	A.U.E.W.S/M 6
" " "	" "	"	T & G.W.U. 8/53
" " "	" "	"	A.U.E.W. S/Moor TASS
" " "	" "	"	T & G.W.U. 8/304
McIntyre M.P.	DURHAM	48	A.U.E.W. S/Moor
" " "	" "	"	T.W.U.
" " "	" "	"	Middlestone LP.
" " "	" "	"	Sedgefield LP.
" " "	" "	"	West Cornforth LP.
" " "	" "	"	Bishop Middleham LP.
" " "	" "	"	Bishop Middleham WS.
McCourt P. W.	CHILTON		Chilton/Windlestone LP.
" " "	" "	"	Chilton/Windlestone WS.
" " "	" "	"	G.M.B.A.T.U. Durham ED S
" " "	" "	"	Tudhoe LP.
Pimlott B.	LONDON		T & G.W.U. 8/20
" " "	" "	"	Trimdon Colliery LP.
" " "	" "	"	T & G.W.U. 8/151 ?
" " "	" "	"	Winterton COHSE
" " "	" "	"	A. U.E.W. 62SE
Race D.A.R.	LONDON	36	N.U.P.E. Winterton
" " "	" "	"	N.U.P.E. Easington
Robson F. S.	DARLINGTON	59	Darlington Rural No. 1
Storey K.	DURHAM	50	P.O.E.U.
Taylor Gooby	PETERLEE	38	N.E. Co-op
Thompson Allen	KELLOE	53	N.U.M. Durham Area
Thompson Derek	WINGATE	52	Wingate LP.
Watkins D.J.	RICHMOND SURREY	58	A.U.E.W.
" "	" "	"	A.U.E.W. 393 SE

SEDGEFIELD CONSTITUENCY LABOUR PARTY.

Secretary :- George Ferguson , 99, Wood Vue Spennymoor. Tel 815007.

To all delegates General Committee.   19 TH /30 TH only
members Executive Committee.   18/19/20

Notice of Meetings

A series of meetings will be held as follows:-

Wednesday 18th May 1983. at 7pm. Spennymoor Town Hall
Executive committee meeting
Agenda :- To consider nominations of
prospective Parliamentary Candidates.
To appoint stewards. To shortlist.

Thursday 19th May 1983. at 7 pm. in Spennymoor Town Hall
General Committee.
Agenda :- To further consider nominations
of prospective Parliamentary Candidates.

, Friday 20th May 1983. at 7 pm. in Spennymoor Town Hall
General Committee.
Agenda :- To select candidate.

Please note :-
Delegates are requested to carry current party
membership cards. Once meeting has started late
comers will not be admitted.

Left: The list of applicants who wanted to become the Labour candidate for the newly-created Sedgefield seat in 1983. *Right:* The time and place of the meetings which decided the candidate

writing, that Tony Blair was the official Trimdon Village Labour Party nominee for candidature in the Sedgefield Constituency in the forthcoming General Election. In return, the CLP secretary George Ferguson gave Burton a handwritten note which stated: "I hereby acknowledge receipt of your nomination in respect of: Anthony Charles Lynton Blair."

The Trimdon Posse, though, was not working entirely alone. Even before his first meeting with Burton and the others, Blair had talked to the Labour MP for Chester-le-Street, Giles Radice, who had put him in touch with Joe Mills, head of the northern region of the Transport and General Workers' Union (TGWU). Blair was a member of this union. Mills was also chairman of the Northern Region Labour Party and was strongly against the selection of Huckfield as the candidate for the Sedgefield seat. Huckfield was on the far left of the party. He had abandoned his seat at Nuneaton because its boundaries had been redrawn so that it was likely to fall to the Conservatives. Now he was searching for a seat in safer Labour territory.

As a member of the TGWU, Huckfield too had approached Mills for support – but Mills had given him a letter noting that he was "a sponsored member of the TGWU" which was patently not the recommendation Huckfield was after.

John Burton: The Grit in the Oyster

Above: The hurriedly mis-typed CV of the candidate "Tony Glair" whose wife came from "Loverpool" – and those who look closely will find other, more embarrassing, mistakes

Instead Mills turned to helping Blair. The TGWU had few branches that were affiliated to Sedgefield CLP, but Mills helped Blair find one at a local public transport company called Trimdon Motor Services. That branch went on to provide Blair's second nomination.

Getting a nomination or two was the easy bit. Now Burton had to persuade the CLP Executive to put Blair on the shortlist from which the May 20 meeting would make its choice.

"The Executive in those days was made up of 13 trade union members and 13 from the constituency," says Burton. "A group of these members, led by Spennymoor Trades' Council, was politically to the far left and was supporting Les Huckfield. Its object was to manipulate the shortlist so that it would be easy for Huckfield to win, so they wanted to put nominees on it who they felt did not have massive support."

The Executive met in Spennymoor Town Hall at seven o'clock on Wednesday, May 18. It had before it Blair's hurriedly-prepared CV. Perhaps because of the typed CV's many errors – it refers to "Tony Glair" and says that his wife Cherie came from "Loverpool" – a shortlist of six was drawn up which did not include Blair: Huckfield, Warren McCourt (Sedgefield District Council leader), Pat

McIntyre (Durham activist), Frank Robson (Darlington councillor), Reg Race (far left former MP) and Bill Giffin (Fire Brigades Union representative). Their names would be put to the General Committee the following evening when the agenda was "to further consider nominations of prospective Parliamentary Candidates".

"I was determined that Tony's name would be added to that list," says Burton. "But at that May 18 meeting, the left on the Executive tried to ensure no other name would be added by mandating the entire Executive to vote against any additions to the list the next night. That meant that 26 people, because all of them would be at Thursday's General Committee meeting, had decided or had been instructed to block any further additions. What they did was completely against Labour Party rules; it was totally wrong."

On Thursday, May 19, promising to meet Lily, Blair and some of the others later in the Red Lion at Trimdon, Burton went to the General Committee meeting in Spennymoor Town Hall, again at seven o'clock, which all delegates were entitled to attend.

This was only the second General Committee Burton had attended, the first having been when the new Sedgefield constituency was formed. However, chatting to people before proceedings began, he quickly realised that many of the delegates were very unhappy about having a shortlist imposed upon them. They were from places like Deaf Hill, Wingate, Thornley and Wheatley Hill which had formerly been part of the Easington or Durham constituency; Burton had been at school with some, and had come across others on his footballing travels. A few were related to Lily. Perhaps he had more allies than he had dared to hope.

And he had a friend in the chair, as in charge of the meeting was the chairman of the CLP, George Terrans. Terrans went through the list of the 16 candidates who had nominations – there had been 17 but Sid Weighell, the former railway union leader, had withdrawn the previous day.

Terrans went down the list alphabetically, asking for reasons why each name should be added to the shortlist. First was Hilary Armstrong, then Joel Barnett – both rejected. Third was Tony Blair. Burton stood up.

"Mr Chairman, I would like to propose that Tony Blair be added to the short list. I have here a letter from Michael Foot thanking Tony for his performance in the Beaconsfield by-election and stating that he would like to see him in the House of Commons as soon as possible."

Another delegate got to his feet to oppose Burton's proposal, arguing that everyone who stood unsuccessfully for Parliament received such a letter. Far from stopping Burton in his tracks, the objector succeeded only in allowing him to extend his argument.

"That's not strictly true, Mr Chairman. The wording in this letter's slightly different and more personal because it acknowledges the help Tony has given Mr Foot with speech writing."

The objector sat down and Burton's proposal was seconded so Terrans put the matter to the vote. Should Tony Blair's name be added to the shortlist? There were three tellers. Bill Waters from Byers Green, as the head teller, gave Terrans the result: the number for adding Blair to the shortlist was 42, the number against was 41.

"Actually," Burton smiles, "Bill came up to me after the meeting and explained that all three tellers had come up with different figures – 42 for Blair, 41 against, 41 for and 41 against, and 41 for with 40 against. He reasoned that since there had been two in Blair's favour and one draw, that preference should be communicated to Terrans."

The chairman continued down the list and, while other additions were suggested, none found a seconder. Terrans then read out the amended shortlist which included the name of Tony Blair.

It was then that a left-wing delegate jumped to his feet and demanded a recount on Blair's inclusion. Terrans refused; the vote had been perfectly fair and the matter was closed, he said. Burton found out later that some of the councillors on the Executive, despite having been firmly instructed to block any additions, had given their votes to Blair.

Scarcely able to contain his joy and excitement, Burton drove back to Trimdon Village, parked his car and went to the Red Lion. Knowing perfectly well that those inside were anxiously awaiting his arrival, he still had to exercise his wicked sense of humour. As he walked in, Lily, Blair, Wilson, Trippett, Brookes and his wife Christine all fell silent.

Brookes asked what the outcome had been. Burton looked despondent and shook his head. "You wouldn't believe it," he said. "They added just one solitary name to the list." He paused. "And that name was Tony Blair."

"It's a moment in time which I'll never forget," Burton says. "There was a split second of silence and then we all went crazy. We'd achieved the impossible.

"Now there was just one more obstacle to be overcome and we were ready for it – the meeting the next night to select the candidate."

Before going to bed on the Thursday night, Burton went quietly to the church of St Mary Magdalene on Trimdon Village green to give thanks for the events of that day and to ask for the strength he would need the next. Unknown to Burton, on the following Friday morning, Blair also quietly took himself to Durham Cathedral to spend some time in prayer.

By 7pm on Friday, May 20, 1983, all seven candidates along with 119 delegates, had gathered in Spennymoor Town Hall. Terrans was again in charge of proceedings. Each candidate would have ten minutes to speak and five to answer questions from the floor.

"Just as the meeting started, the delegate who had spoken so forcefully the previous evening against Tony's inclusion on the shortlist got up yet again," says Burton, shaking his head. "I just couldn't believe it! He went on complaining about Tony being there and, in doing so, repeated Tony's links with the leader of the Labour Party. All he succeeded in doing was heightening Tony's profile at the very start of the meeting."

Almost all who were present agree that Blair spoke brilliantly and answered his questions well. However, a NUPE delegate, Ron Mohon, approached Burton after Blair's performance and said he thought his man had blown his chance by arguing that Britain should be in Europe instead of staying out. Burton disagreed: despite Labour's official policy, Burton thought the mood in the party was changing.

When it came to Huckfield's turn to answer questions, Burton was ready. Joe Mills of the TGWU had provided him with three questions. The tactic was to link Huckfield with the far-left Militant group and to suggest that Labour could not now win Nuneaton because he, Huckfield, had deserted his post.

The vote, when it came, went to five rounds. At the end of the first, Blair gained the highest number of votes, 39, while Frank Robson was eliminated with just five. Round two saw the departure of Bill Giffin and Reg Race. Warren McCourt bowed out in round three and round four wiped out Pat McIntyre. Then there were two.

In the final vote, Huckfield had 46 supporters while Blair romped home with 73. "One of the funniest aspects of the outcome," Burton recalls, "was that George Terrans announced to the assembled delegates that the Sedgefield Parliamentary Constituency now had a Labour Party candidate to contest its first election, less than three weeks away, but he forgot to say who that candidate was. It only became clear when he referred to this person as being a bright young chap. Then we knew."

Against every prediction and beating all the odds, Tony Blair, John Burton and the rest of the Trimdon Posse had achieved the unachievable. "I still can't make my mind up whether or not it was a miracle, as some have suggested," Burton reflects, "but somebody was certainly smiling on us and if it wasn't a miracle then it was definitely the next best thing. Life would never be the same again for any of us and there were even greater changes just over the horizon."

9: I thank you for your voices

THE battle to win the Sedgefield Parliamentary seat for Tony Blair began on the evening he was selected as the constituency's Labour candidate.

Even though this was the Labour-dominated North-East of England, he and his team knew that it was not going to be an easy campaign. If John Burton had thought for one fleeting moment that, having successfully engineered Blair's selection, he could retire to a back seat and retreat to his role as a teacher and a district councillor, he could not have been more wrong.

Sedgefield was a new seat and the Labour Party had little election machinery in place but there was a lot of wisdom and experience readily to hand. It is customary for the candidate to choose his election agent but, with polling day just two-and-a-half weeks away, the local executive committee decided that George Ferguson, the constituency secretary, should take on the role – even though he did not have enough available time to fulfil the agent's duties.

As Burton explains, Ferguson helped greatly and retained the title of agent. But it again fell to Burton and the rest of the 'Famous Five' to plan Blair's frenetic campaign. Their enthusiasm for the job was as intense as ever even though they knew that the Labour Party nationally would not win the 1983 General Election. It was the year when the party's manifesto was described by Gerald Kaufman as "the longest suicide note in history".

"We knew that the manifesto was a disaster," says Burton. "I remember going canvassing along a street in Tudhoe and when I got to the end of it I told Tony that I'd explained eight different defence policies because the party line we were supposed to describe, unilateral nuclear disarmament, was just an absolute disaster. And that policy was one of those which lost us the election. I reached the stage of asking voters what they wanted our defence policy to be and, if it was anything like sensible, agreeing with their view."

Still, though, the 'Famous Five' persevered. Shopping centres, Women's Institutes, Mothers' Unions and workingmen's clubs were the ideal evening venues for people to meet Tony Blair. The days were spent knocking on doors and just talking to people.

Burton remembers how the constituency took to Blair. "All sorts of people were excited by him and were saying that the new constituency had not this time had a candidate imposed on it by the National Union of Mineworkers," he says. "In the past, that's what local people had had to put up with. Here, instead, was a young, intelligent barrister, well-connected and with a degree from Oxford University. People in the constituency just couldn't believe their luck. He was a breath of fresh air and he was made very welcome everywhere he went – well, almost everywhere. I say that because there was one incident during the campaign which is hilarious in retrospect but wasn't funny at the time.

"George Ferguson had decided that, to make sure Tony was noticed when he was travelling about, he needed a distinctive mode of transport. An open-backed Land Rover was suggested and George agreed – just as long as it was colourful, not khaki or grey. The vehicle which arrived was blue, not RAF blue but bright, and I do mean very bright, blue. It was the last thing a prospective Labour MP needed so we did our best to cover as much of it as possible with stickers and the like.

"Then, on the last evening of campaigning, George organised a Labour Party cavalcade of some 20 cars and we planned its intended route around the constituency. It all went well until we got to Wellfield Road at the top end of Wingate. I still don't know exactly how it happened but, for some reason, the lead vehicle turned into a cul-de-sac and, of course, we all followed.

"Just try to imagine it – 20-odd vehicles all plastered with Labour Party stickers. There was no way to turn round, no obvious exit and we came to a stop outside one of the few houses displaying Conservative Party posters. I'm sure the poor woman who lived there was convinced that she was under attack, that we'd descended on her en masse to exact revenge because she'd dared to do such a thing.

"Councillor Margaret Courtney-Shaw, one of Tony's most fervent supporters, was sitting next to him, enthusing to anyone who would listen about this Oxford graduate, 'such a gentle, refined young man with lovely manners'.

"Tony suddenly realised what was happening, leapt to his feet and asked loudly: 'Which stupid bugger organised this fiasco?' Because his microphone was still switched on, his words were relayed to everyone whose ears the loudspeaker reached. I thought poor Mrs Courtney-Shaw was going to faint and we didn't have any smelling salts handy!

"It took us the top side of 15 minutes to get all the vehicles out of that street but Tony, seeing the funny side, as he always does, took it all in good part."

Blair was also highly amused during the campaign when one morning, on answering the door of the Burtons' house where he was staying, he found on the step the Conservative candidate who, almost without looking up from his list, asked if he could be relied on to support the Tories. Blair's reply was polite but in the negative.

"Throughout the whole campaign," Burton remembers, "Tony just generated this atmosphere of friendliness in what wasn't really a friendly campaign nationally. There was a lot of back-biting, people were getting at one another, the Left was pushing its way forward and being extreme. It was an election that we knew the Labour Party hadn't a hope of winning but we wanted to do well in Sedgefield, particularly with it being a new constituency. The difference around here was that we had a sense of humour, we got on with people, we were trying to take the argument out of politics but, nevertheless, push forward the Labour Party's views and we succeeded in doing that.

"There was no doubt that Labour was going to win the Sedgefield seat but Tony wanted to win well, not just for himself but for us – we who had taken up this strange body, an Oxford educated barrister. And he did win well, completely vindicating our faith in him.

"During the campaign, we took some flak from those on the Left but the real people of the area, the man and woman in the street, had no problem at all with Tony's background or his accent. They were happy to embrace him and were supportive of what he wanted to do.

"They were ready for change. They'd already learned how to manage change; the mines were closing and they'd coped with that. They knew that they could handle change and that is one of the main reasons, I believe, that New Labour was able to start here. The people wanted someone who would really represent them, give them, in time, what they wanted. Tony talked continuously about care and compassion and that's what socialism should be all about. Right wing and Left wing don't come into that philosophy; it's purely about helping people."

Coronation Street star Pat Phoenix, who played Elsie Tanner in the television series and was a close friend of Cherie Blair's father, Tony Booth, also came to Sedgefield to lend her support to the campaign. The village of West Cornforth had its own, real, Coronation Street and beneath its sign she posed with Blair. Lily Burton then travelled with her by car to Wingate and recounts that Pat was "absolutely charming", even though she was in a rush to get back to the Granada Studios in Manchester.

"With what time she had, we took her round a home for the elderly in Wingate and then somebody pointed out that there was another old people's home in the village too and that there'd be a deal of trouble if 'Elsie Tanner' visited one and not the other," says Burton. "It was a fair point.

"I kept an eye on the time as I was conscious that she needed to get away. She was really wonderful with the old people, lovely. I went up to her and said quietly, 'Pat, I'm sorry about the extra time here and I know it puts you in a bit of a rush for Manchester but it wasn't Tony Blair's fault, it was mine. I'm really sorry.' As agent, I had to take the blame, didn't I? She turned round to me, continued smiling and said through gritted teeth but still with a perfect smile, 'You bastard.' She wasn't being unpleasant. It was her idea of a pithy response but just for a moment she became Elsie Tanner and I felt like Len Fairclough or someone else from Coronation Street feeling the sharp end of her tongue.

"She'd campaigned for Tony in the 1982 Beaconsfield by-election and liked him a lot although, by her own admission, she didn't have a lot of time for either politics or politicians."

In 1983, Newton Aycliffe was not in the Sedgefield constituency; it was within Bishop Auckland's boundaries, but it was at the Aycliffe Leisure Centre that the counts for both seats took place on election night.

"The first ballot boxes that began to arrive were, for obvious reasons, from those places nearest to Newton Aycliffe where the count was being held while the last to come in were from areas furthest afield," remembers Burton. "But, as they were stacked up, the latest to arrive were at the top and they were the first to be opened, the ones from the country villages of Hurworth, Neasham, Piercebridge, High Coniscliffe, Low Coniscliffe and so on. These were the more rural parts of the constituency around Darlington which were certainly less Labour than most of the other parts.

"The ballot papers from these places indicated that the vote was about 50/50 and Tony started to panic. It was absolute panic and I remember Stan Haswell, a headteacher and Labour councillor, telling me not to worry as he'd 'sort the young man out'. I didn't realise what was going on but he took Tony away with him down the stairs and gave him a whisky.

"When the lower boxes were eventually opened, the situation changed rapidly but Tony continued to worry despite the reassurances he was being given. I was walking around keeping an eye on the count, which is what I was supposed to do. It was soon very obvious that everything was fine, as I'd told him it would be but he wasn't convinced until the returning officer made the declaration."

The result confirmed Burton's faith:

ACL Blair (Labour)	21,401
GTAW Horton (Conservative)	13,120
DL Shand (SDP)	10,183
ME Logan-Salton (Independent)	298

Blair's majority was a comfortable 8,281.

A new kind of Labour Member of Parliament had been elected to represent the new constituency of Sedgefield and the repercussions, which could not possibly have been foreseen at the time, were gradually to change forever not just the Labour movement but the entire face of British politics.

Blair and Burton left the leisure centre for Trimdon Village.

John Burton: The Grit in the Oyster

"It was while I was driving him back that Tony said to me: 'I'll only say this once; I'll never, ever, be able to repay you for what you've done.' He's never mentioned it since and I've never wanted him to," says Burton. "That's the way we are – good friends. He doesn't have to repay me for what I've done but he has done so by his company and his friendship."

They arrived at The Red Lion, which had been so strategically important to their campaign, where the whole team had a party and the landlord and landlady, Maureen and Norman, had laid on some food.

"When had we last eaten?" Burton asks. "I've no idea! Food was irrelevant that day. I don't think any of us ate anything. We must have done, I suppose, but I can't remember where, what or when."

Tony's father Leo, was there. In the late 1950s, Leo had brought his young family back from Australia because he wanted to stand for Parliament – as a Tory. By 1964, Leo was a law lecturer at Durham University, a barrister practising in Newcastle and chairman of the Durham Conservative Association. Just as he was at the height of his powers and ready to find a seat, Leo was struck down by a stroke. He wasn't able to speak for three years and his cruel fate undoubtedly spurred his son on. Now, in 1983, he saw his son succeed where illness had prevented him.

"Leo was tremendously excited and kept coming up to me to tell me how grateful he was that I'd done this for his son, that it would never have happened had it not been for me," says Burton. " I replied that all I'd done was to support Tony and that what he'd achieved he'd done by himself. He's always been very kind to me and that night he was overjoyed at the outcome. It didn't matter in the slightest that Tony had become a Labour MP. He was just so proud of what his son had achieved. At that time, Leo was a Tory and the Labour Party was a million miles away from him but we knew that it had to change and I'm sure that he thought that if his son had any influence in the future he would do something to try to change it."

The party went on until four in the morning. There was much to celebrate; all that had come to pass had been achieved within some four short weeks.

"Tony's never been one to drink too much and, despite having had the greatest excuse in his life to date to do so, he had 'just the one'; he does enjoy a drink but he did have, honestly, just the one. Some of us might have had a couple more but the memory of that entire night remains crystal clear for us all. How could anyone forget such an occasion? It's etched there, forever, and the atmosphere, the elation, can never be conveyed in mere words."

During the night, Tony telephoned Cherie who was contesting the seat of Thanet North in Kent. She was unsuccessful, coming third and only just saving her deposit but she was delighted by her husband's news.

"You wouldn't believe just how long it took to sink in for all of us who were involved," says Burton. "We'd started this once-upon-a-time fairytale and, against all odds, it had come true. None of us could believe that it had really happened."

After that evening, that day which went so quickly and yet seemed to go on forever, it was down to work for the new MP. He had gained a passport to a whole new world. He had a good idea of what constituency and Parliamentary business was all about but the reality of it all was something else.

While to many this was the end of the Burton/Blair story, to other, more astute, observers, those who dared look beyond the political horizon, it was no more than the first chapter in what would be an on-going saga.

10: A round, unvarnished tale

IMMEDIATELY after the 1983 election, Tony Blair appointed John Burton as his official election agent. It is a job which only exists when an election is imminent, although between campaigns most agents keep a low profile and a weather eye on matters in the constituency while the MP is away at Westminster.

The role kept Burton in touch with nearly everything in which the newly-appointed Member of Parliament was involved. He accompanied Blair on most of his weekly three-hour-long Saturday surgery 'rounds', and on many of his visits to the towns and villages of the rural constituency.

They also travelled further afield together including one evening to a meeting of the Fabian Society in Newcastle-upon-Tyne where Blair had been invited to speak.

"We had to park at the station and walk to the hotel just across the road," says Burton. "I've got 'footballer's legs' and, throughout my adult life, I've accidentally torn more pairs of trousers, usually at the most inopportune times, than you could believe. This was yet another of those occasions.

"As I got out of the car, my trousers snagged on the door lock catch and, when I looked, I hadn't this time just torn the seam of my trousers; I'd ripped them right across the back so badly that my underwear was on public display. Fortunately, there was nobody around to see but I told Tony that, given the circumstances, I couldn't possibly go with him into the meeting. I didn't even have an overcoat with me with which to cover my embarrassment.

"He, however, couldn't see that there would be any real problem and insisted that I went with him. He would walk behind me, he said, and that would solve the problem. Not totally convinced, I went along with his idea. As we walked across to the hotel, it looked as though his ploy was working but then we had to traverse the foyer and climb a long, curved staircase. Tony continued to guard my rear, if I can say that, as making my way up I sidled, sideways, along the wall.

"As Tony was being introduced to this person and that, I stood bolt upright, my back against the nearest wall. My worst imaginings took over my mind; I began to panic and explained quietly to Tony that I'd have to go into the toilets to see if the damage was as bad as I believed it to be.

"Excusing himself to his hosts on the grounds that he wanted to wash his face, he walked behind me to the nearest facilities. We soon found that the tear was virtually irreparable and then I got the giggles – and when I start it is usually a long time before I can stop. He asked what the matter was and when I eventually recovered something of my composure, I replied: 'You've just leaned over to see how bad it is. If a newspaper photographer had walked in at that moment with you peering at my backside, I think it's a fair bet that we'd have hit every front page in the country, if not the world!' We then both dissolved into fits of laughter and I spent the meeting sitting, carefully, in the back row.

"While I continued to worry about how we'd get back to the car, he made a superb speech as if there was nothing at all wrong. I was delighted, however, when he opted not to stay on for coffee. He must have seen the look on my face when he was invited to do so."

Phil Wilson had left his job at the National Savings offices in Durham to work full time for the new MP and John Burton recruited Margaret Thomas to be Blair's secretary. Blair, then the youngest MP in the Parliamentary Labour Party, spent most of his time in London. He shared an allocated office first with the Militant Dave Nellist and then, a short time later, with Gordon Brown. But, as he had promised those who had supported his candidacy, he found plenty of time to keep in touch with his constituency.

Blair made his maiden speech to the House of Commons on July 6, 1983, less than a month after his election. In it, speaking out against the high level of unemployment and reinforcing the views he had laid out before his constituents in Sedgefield, he said: "I am a socialist not through reading a textbook that has caught my intellectual fancy, nor through unthinking tradition, but because I believe that, at its best, socialism corresponds most closely to an existence that is both rational and moral.

"It stands for co-operation, not confrontation, for fellowship and not fear. It stands for equality, not because it wants people to be the same but because only through equality in our economic circumstances can our individuality develop properly."

At Westminster, Blair's talents were quickly recognised. By 1985 Neil Kinnock, who had become leader of the Labour Party on October 2, 1983, following the resignation of Michael Foot, had promoted him to Labour's Treasury front bench team.

He was also moving up in Sedgefield. On his frequent visits to the constituency, he stayed with the Burtons, Caroline giving up her room for him. But in late 1984, after scouring Sedgefield village and West Cornforth, the Blairs found a place of their own.

To be precise, Peter Brookes inadvertently found it for them. He was looking for a bigger home and had commissioned a survey on Myrobella House in Trimdon Colliery. Then he decided that it was not right for his family and so suggested to Blair that it might fulfil his needs.

Blair went to see it and liked it immediately, as did Cherie, despite the fact that it was not then centrally heated. It was ideally situated, almost in the middle of the constituency and, although it was in a former colliery village, it had fields on two sides. Blair saw the estate agent, used Brookes' survey and placed his sealed bid which was successful. The Blairs had a home in the north.

"Isn't it funny!" says Burton, his eyes lighting up. "I became a PE teacher not just because I was good at sport but also because I'd been greatly influenced by my PE teacher at grammar school, Bill Saunders. By sheer coincidence, Bill was the executor for the estate of which that house was a part.

"Contrary to popular belief, Myrobella was never a colliery manager's house but always a family home built in 1898 for the Carter family. Years earlier, Lily had gone there for some of her piano lessons. The house name comes from the Myrobella plum trees which still grow in the garden. The Victorians apparently loved to make preserves with the fruit but you never hear them mentioned now."

The removal did not go too smoothly but that was not the fault of the removers. "We got Griersons to move the Blairs," says Burton. "Everything was loaded carefully into the back of their wagon and then we all climbed in too. As we were going through Trimdon Grange, something flew out of the back but nobody saw what it was and we didn't bother to stop.

"After we had unpacked everything at the house, Cherie was looking frantically for her Victorian lamp. It wasn't anywhere at Myrobella so we went back and searched our house, but it wasn't there either. We didn't dare tell her, and she still doesn't know, that it was her Victorian lamp which parted company with the wagon in Trimdon Grange. Somebody there has the Prime Minister's wife's lamp and I bet she'd like it back."

In 1987, Blair was made Labour's spokesperson on Trade and Industry with special responsibility for consumer affairs and the City. In 1988, having been elected to the Shadow Cabinet, he became Shadow Secretary of State for Energy then, in 1989, Shadow Secretary of State for Employment, in which role he forged a new industrial relations policy which ended Labour's support for the 'closed shop'.

Many of his ideas at Employment were shaped by his experiences in Sedgefield, parts of which endured more than 20 per cent unemployment. One of those parts was the village of Fishburn, and the newly-elected Blair's first campaign had been to save its cokeworks – and 273 jobs – from closure.

The first campaign, directly after the 1983 election, had been moderately successful in that it granted Fishburn a stay of execution until 1986. But as Blair and Burton worked to save the old industry, they began to realise that the people had new aspirations.

Said Blair: "I remember in 1986 a local councillor coming up to me and saying: 'It's very good of you to do all this, Mr Blair, but the people are fed up with the factory'."

Burton remembers: "We said that while we were fighting to keep open industries such as and we were building the barricades, the workers were doing their best to pull them down.

"A lot of them wanted to be out and to take the redundancy money on offer. We were saying that the business employed a lot of people and that the redundancy on offer wasn't very much. It might have seemed like a lot of money but in reality it wasn't – just enough for a three-piece suite or something like that.

"We managed to keep the place open at first but after that, the second time, when it closed, it just wasn't worth running the campaign because people's attitudes had changed. People wanted to get out of those industries and into what was on offer on the new factory sites. We could see that change; we'd seen it in 1983. The coal and steel industries were declining and people were changing. The cokeworks was one of the last things in the process. People just didn't want it any more. They were ready for new industry."

They were probably also ready for New Labour, but despite Kinnock's reforming leadership, Labour lost the 1987 General Election. Burton argues diplomatically that although Kinnock did an excellent job, not enough progress had been made in modernising the party and turning it into the New Labour that the Sedgefield constituents were looking for. The mountain which the party on a national level had to climb was too steep and too high.

"The truth is that we never thought that we'd win in 1987," says Burton. "We were coming from too far behind. We'd suffered a massive defeat in 1983 under Michael Foot's leadership, 'the longest suicide note in history' and all that, and major changes had to be made. Kinnock had started to make them, there's no question about that. He was changing policies, such as unilateral nuclear disarmament and renationalisation, which weren't acceptable to the electorate. He was getting around to taking on Militant and removing them from the party because he knew full well that the nation wouldn't elect a party of extremes – and we were then still perceived as being extremely to the left. He had led the party to abandon its 1983 vow to withdraw Britain from the European Community.

"Nevertheless, it was obvious that the changes weren't going to work in time for that 1987 election. I knew that we weren't going to win. We were still deemed unfit to govern and so many people continued to be content with Margaret Thatcher's record as Prime Minister. The philosophy of 'the community' prospering, ergo the individual, sponsored later by Tony, had not yet emerged and so the 'I'm alright Jack and bugger everybody else' mentality still held sway.

John Burton: The Grit in the Oyster

"The Falklands War, although it had been fought five years earlier, had strengthened the perception of Thatcher as 'The Iron Lady'. Kinnock was leading the Labour Party in the right direction. To this day, Tony always acknowledges just how important Kinnock's leadership was to him. He wouldn't have been Prime Minister if Kinnock hadn't put these changes into motion.

"Kinnock believed in the need for change and the wheels for it were turning, but they were still doing so only slowly. In 1989 the party gave up its determination to implement unilateral nuclear disarmament if it came to power."

That change came in time for the 1992 General Election when John Major was the Conservative Prime Minister following Mrs Thatcher's resignation in 1990. Labour was close to victory and yet, with an eventual overall Conservative majority of 21 seats, not a huge margin, still so far away from government.

"Tony thought that we'd lose by about 20 seats and his estimate was just one out. That was a pretty accurate forecast by any standard, quite staggering really," says Burton who had entered the campaign more positively. "But we both knew that the changes had to go on.

"I felt that there were several reasons for our defeat. I noticed one in the build-up to the election. It was a last minute thing, actually. With Tony, I was going around the Rothman's tobacco factory at Spennymoor, a town which was then in our Sedgefield constituency. Our Shadow Chancellor John Smith had stated that the higher rate of tax would be introduced on incomes of £24,000. As a teacher, and a head of department at that, I couldn't personally foresee a time when I would be earning anything even approaching £20,000 but, as we walked around giving out Labour Party badges and stickers to people who had, traditionally and actually, always voted Labour, I was approached by a man who asked: 'John, about this higher level of tax. What's your view?'

"I told him my personal circumstances and he replied by saying that he already earned over £24,000 a year on the shop-floor at Rothman's and that his wife, pointing to her just a few yards away, was paid almost as much.

"And then he said a very interesting thing. 'Don't forget that if you're earning £20,000, you want to earn £24,000.' And I thought that he was so right and it was then that it hit me. I'm sure that that tax policy was one of the reasons that we lost the election. Anybody who was doing reasonably well, anybody who was aspiring to do reasonably well was always considering the 'pound in your pocket'. It was then I realised that this was going to be a major election issue – and it was."

The small details of the taxation of the private individual may have been an error. But there was also a glaringly public mistake that contributed to the defeat.

"Earlier in the campaign, there had been the Labour rally at Sheffield with an audience of 10,000 party stalwarts," continues Burton.

"Tony went down from Sedgefield to join the shadow cabinet on the platform. Neil Kinnock flew in by helicopter. After all the frenetic build-up by singers and celebrities, Neil walked onto that platform, almost mobbed as he walked from the back of the huge hall, down the central aisle through the audience and, as he reached the microphones, he gesticulated and voiced, loudly, 'We're alright! We're alright!' He just went completely over the top.

"Peter Mandelson, also on the platform, leaned forward and said, quietly, to Tony and Gordon (Brown): 'We've just lost the election!'

"I was watching that rally at home on television. I could have gone down to it with Tony but, for a number of reasons, I didn't. I watched it, the frenzy, saw what happened and, despite my personal misgivings, tried to dismiss the whole thing believing that, at the end of the day, everything would turn out alright. But, at the back of my mind, there was an innate belief that this had gone completely over the top. These were not the actions of a dignified person who would lead the country as prime minister. Neil says now that he did it, that he realised that he was doing it but that he couldn't stop himself from doing it. He also knew, he says, that it was the wrong thing to do. It was a gesture, he says, to his supporters within the room but the event was being broadcast nationally to people who weren't, necessarily, his supporters. I saw it as an almost hysterical, rally, the opposite of dignified politics.

"It was totally out of character for Neil. He'd worked so hard to change the party and is such a good man and a clever one. He would have made a good leader for the country. There's no question about that in my mind but it was still possible to 'blow it' in a minute or two – and we did. There were still doubts in many other people's minds about whether Neil was up to being prime minister and a lot saw the rally as indicating that he wasn't. How is history made, eh? Things like that."

In April 1992, following the defeat, Kinnock stepped down. "The changes had to go on," Burton says swiftly. "The annual conference was largely dominated by members slagging off their own party. You get a week's television coverage. How often do you get an opportunity like that? If it had to be paid for, it would cost a fortune and we, the Labour Party, were seen on television arguing with one another. The whole thing was farcical. Of course we need debate and discussion but we most certainly don't want the open warfare we used to have. That had to change."

In 1992 Blair was elected to Labour's National Executive Committee, the party's ruling body, and the new Labour leader, John Smith, appointed him as Shadow Home Secretary. In September of that year, along with John Prescott, Blair led the drive to turn Labour into a mass-membership party.

That drive had its roots in Sedgefield in general and Trimdon Village in particular where Burton had long tried to entice anyone into local Labour meetings in the hope that they might join the party.

In 1993, something else happened in the village which would one day turn the global spotlight upon it, but at the time was more about encouraging ordinary people to become Labour members. It was the formation of the Sedgefield Constituency Labour (Trimdon) Club Limited.

"Until it was set up," Burton looks back, "constituency meetings and a number of other Labour events had been held a few miles down the road in Fishburn Working Men's Club, an arrangement which worked fairly well except that women weren't allowed in the bar and couldn't be full members so we got a lot of justifiable moans about that. Also we had to ask the club committee whenever we wanted to do anything there. The answer was almost always that we could and they were always more than helpful but we felt that we needed something more, something that we could call our own but we didn't have a lot of money to create such a place.

"Then something happened which was unfortunate but which made it possible for our dream to become a reality: Trimdon Village Working Men's Club went into receivership. Paul Trippett was the steward there and he came to tell me what was going on and how the club was losing £57 a week. He believed that, under a revised form of management and working in a different way and with different staffing arrangements, the finances could be significantly improved."

On July 9, 1993, The Northern Echo reported the changing of the guard at the club. It said: "Today sees the end of an era for Trimdon Village as the struggling workingmen's club finally shuts down after 74 years. In its heyday the busy club reflected thriving village life, when collieries provided plenty of work for local men and the community flourished. But for the past five years it has been operating under receivership after folding in the 1980s amid rumours and a police investigation into its finances.

"Despite its inglorious end, the club, which began with a single barrel of beer in farm workers' cottages in 1919, will be remembered by many as once an integral part of village life. Mick Terrans, a club committee member for 14 years, remembers the institution it was.

"'It survived a major fire and debt problems and by the start of World War Two it had £10,000 profits,' said Mr Terrans, who retired as a long-serving county councillor in May and was awarded the OBE this year. 'In 1952 the Front Street cottages were demolished and a new £30,000 club built and it went from strength to strength. It was a smashing club, very important to local people. It will have a treasured place in people's memories. But when they closed the collieries things started to go downhill.'

"In 1985 the club let women in for the first time but even that failed to restore its vitality.

"Although the WMC has closed, its building will continue as a social centre. Sedgefield Constituency Labour Party has leased the club from the Federation Brewery and tonight holds a fundraising event with guest VIPs Neil and Glenys Kinnock. The sell-out party includes entertainment by Alan Price.'

The next day's paper carried a follow-up report which included a foretaste of the many significant political speeches which would be made at the Trimdon Village venue:

"Neil Kinnock helped launch a new Labour club in County Durham last night, saying it was a sign of the vitality being stirred in the party across the nation. Sedgefield Constituency Labour Club took over the workingmen's club building at Trimdon Village with a night of celebration as more than 300 people packed into the newly decorated hall.

"And the glittering event not only marked a new era for the club building, but the tenth anniversary of MP Tony Blair's election to the Sedgefield constituency.

"Mr Blair, shadow Home Secretary, said Mr Kinnock had breathed new life into the Labour Party during his time as leader and was helping bring new life to the club.

"Mr Blair also said Neil Kinnock had inspired him to go into politics and he would go down in history as one of the great political leaders of our time.

"Mr Kinnock, accompanied by his wife Glenys, said: 'This club has been taken over in the name of the people, it will be run for the people and it will exist for the advance of the people.'

"He also referred to the present controversy within the Party over the one member-one vote issue: 'There can never be any question of putting asunder the Party and trade unions,' said Mr Kinnock. 'Our problem is not turkeys voting for Christmas, but ostriches burying their heads. We need democracy with strength, unity and vitality.'

"Chairman of the constituency party and the new club, John Burton, said: 'It's a big night for Sedgefield and part of a mass membership drive here. We already have 1,700 constituency members and this club is going to help us to keep in touch with the people.'"

Burton remembers the time with affection. "Paul Trippett was right," he says.

John Burton: The Grit in the Oyster

"The old club had been taking about £1,700 per week and within a couple of weeks of us taking over that figure became about £5,000. We redecorated the entrance area, refurbished the toilets, borrowing money from the Federation Brewery.

"I'm grandly called president of the club. Now we can hold meetings whenever we like and arrange whatever functions we want without asking anyone. We have a very nice bar and a superb function room as well as offices. Tony loves the place itself as well as for the fact that it's a focal point for his constituency."

Indeed, in 1998, when Tony Blair had become Prime Minister, he took his French counterpart, Lionel Jospin, to "his club" to meet some of his constituents.

Following the opening of the club, Burton's working relationship with Blair changed. Since Blair's chaotic election in 1983, Burton had remained as his agent – an informal position inbetween elections.

"I was still working on his behalf in the constituency but was also teaching at Sedgefield," Burton says. "The trouble was that my health wasn't as good as it had been and all the years of playing football in all weathers had taken their toll. I was suffering badly from arthritis and just couldn't go on. I was having to drag myself onto the playing field and the basketball court. I was frequently in a lot of pain and some days it was almost unbearable. There was even a period of time when the doctors thought that I might have heart problems too but, thankfully, that proved not to be the case. However, it was clear that I was going to have to retire from teaching."

Burton's health problems coincided with Phil Wilson, Blair's researcher and political assistant since 1983, getting itchy feet.

"Phil had done a superb job in the constituency but felt that the time had come to move on so he went to work for the party nationally at Walworth Road in London," says Burton. "Tony had to find somebody to replace him so I proposed that although I was no longer up to the physical side of being a PE teacher and was about to retire I was more than capable of sitting, thinking and answering letters, which is an integral part of the job in an MP's office. I also explained that knowing people in the constituency so well would further equip me for the job Phil was leaving.

"Frankly, Tony wasn't too sure whether an arrangement like that would work since we'd been such good friends for over ten years. He thought that my working for him might change our relationship in a way that neither of us would want. I acknowledged his reservations but suggested that we could give it a try. So we did.

"That was in April 1994. I'm still here and we're still the firmest of friends. To be truthful, we've never had a crossed word but I've always, as he would wish, given my own honest opinion on everything on which he's asked me to make a judgement. To have done anything less would have been a betrayal of his trust in me and I can truly say that I would never do that – and Tony knows it."

11: Such stuff as dreams are made on

ON May 12, 1994, John Smith, the leader of the Labour Party, died suddenly.

"We were all devastated," says John Burton, the newly-appointed political assistant to the Shadow Home Secretary, Tony Blair.

"It was so sad. I remember when John visited the Sedgefield constituency. He'd spoken at a May Day rally in Thornley and then came back to Trimdon. It was a fine day and there was a small gathering on Peter Brookes' lawn. When he was asked what he would like to drink, he asked what there was. 'We've got red wine or brown ale,' he was told. 'I somehow knew,' he replied, 'that Sedgefield was a brown ale and claret sort of place.'"

For Burton, and Blair, life would never be the same again.

"The whole world changed overnight," says Burton. "The phones in the office and at home never stopped ringing with calls. They were phoning up Tony, and I was answering. Peter Mandelson, Gordon Brown, Margaret Beckett, John Prescott, the newspapers, the media – everybody.

"Would he support this person or that one? Was he going to run himself? Was he going to stand against Brown?

"Being a politician, I said: 'Now is not the time to talk about these things. Our prayers and thoughts must be with the Smith family at such a devastating time.' We were all genuinely gobsmacked."

Yet the Westminster village was far from gobsmacked. In fact, it was consumed by gossip. The leader was dead. Long live the leader – but who was that leader to be?

Smith's death presented Blair with the biggest dilemma of his political life so far. He'd been elected in the dog days of 1983 and had shared an office in Westminster with that intake's other bright young thing, Gordon Brown. But Brown had always been the brighter hope of the pair. He'd already reached the lofty office of Shadow Chancellor of the Exchequer and it had long been assumed – by Brown, by Blair and by political commentators – that it would be the Dunfermline East MP who would one day make it to be leader.

Yet, almost imperceptibly, over the previous two years, people had started to question this assumption. Blair had grown visibly: his improving stature in the public eye and his winning telegenetic smile in the camera's eye had all been noticed.

Burton saw it, and one day, long before Smith's death, he had suggested as much to Blair. Burton remembers that he and Blair were talking alone amid a group of people walking somewhere along the North-East coast when he first raised it.

"We were talking about how the party was improving," recalls Burton. "We were always discussing the changes and whether things were getting better, and I was saying it was all about the way the party was perceived by Middle England. I said: 'Jim Callaghan was Welsh, Michael Foot was Welsh, Neil Kinnock was Welsh, and John Smith is Scottish. I don't want to be racist about this, but the electorate is more liable to accept an English leader.'

"He laughed and said: 'But I'm Scottish, I was born in Scotland.' But I said that he wasn't perceived as being Scottish.

"And then I said as we were walking along: 'You know, you are going to have to lead this party.' It didn't look like it had occurred to him.

"Looking back, I don't think he had any ambition to be leader. Of course when you get to Tony's level you do have ambition but it wasn't the be all and end all for him. The reason he was in politics was not to lead the Labour Party or to be Prime Minister. The be all and end all for him was to see the Labour Party doing something for the country, and to change the party so it could do something for the country."

Plus, of course, there was always Brown acting as a block on any ambitions Blair dared allow himself.

"In the years before, he always thought that Gordon was the one with the ambition, Gordon was the one who had almost worked out a path that would lead him to eventually become leader, Gordon was the dominant figure. So to Tony it was always a case of 'I'm doing very well in politics' and, as he got on – gets on – with Gordon very well, that was always acceptable to Tony.

"Until that day when I said that to him. The way he stopped and looked and said: 'What do you mean?' – it clearly was a surprise to him. He stopped, looked at me almost as if I'd lost my marbles and then walked on ahead. He hardly answered me and I knew then, and I firmly believe, that until then the thought had genuinely never even crossed his mind."

Of course talking of Tony as a future leader was purely hypothetical speculation, because no one could possibly imagine that such a tragic event would put the theories to the test.

But suddenly, out of the blue, the test arose. In the full glare of the media, against the backdrop of a failing Conservative administration, and while desperately trying to mourn the death of a close colleague, Blair and Brown, and their respective camps, had to work out which of them would carry the moderniser's flag into the leadership battle.

"I don't know anything about 'the deal' between the two of them," says

Burton. "I honestly don't. The only meeting I know about was right at the start of the leadership campaign and was a secret meeting at County Hall."

It took place in the office of Kingsley Smith, the chief executive of Durham County Council – "he still says that he was kicked out of his own office while a little bit of history was made". Brown was delivered from Durham Railway Station to the back of County Hall, Burton ushered Blair in through the front door and accompanied him to the chief executive's suite.

"I just left him," says Burton. "It wasn't my place to be in on that."

The outcome of the meeting was quite amicable: whoever was the strongest after a fortnight would continue in the leadership race while the other would drop out. According to this version of events, Blair and Brown's much-vaunted meal at the Granita restaurant in Islington on May 31, 1994, was just to rubber-stamp the deal which had been agreed at Durham two weeks' earlier. That rubber-stamping exercise meant Brown dropping out as the polls showed he had fallen behind during the short campaign.

"Gordon blames Peter Mandelson for making Blair look the strongest during that fortnight but I don't know of any evidence for that," says Burton. "I don't think Peter purposely pushed Blair higher up in the polls, I just think it was inevitable. It was Tony's Englishness, and the fact that the party still needed big change and Blair was the fresh face of socialism. I don't think it took Mandelson to help him, it was inevitable, although the relationship between Gordon and Peter has never been the same since then."

And so the name of Anthony Charles Lynton Blair was put before the four million members of the Labour Party. It was placed alongside those of John Prescott and Margaret Beckett, with Brown left to brood in the background.

Blair began his campaign on June 11 with a speech at Trimdon Labour Club – the first time the club had been in the eye of the national and international media.

"I remember Peter Brookes being interviewed on camera and he was talking about Trimdon being a perfectly normal village with the same problems as anywhere else – which was true as it had high unemployment and was eligible for special grants," says Burton.

"But it was a beautiful sunny day, and someone trotted by on a horse and Peter remembers thinking as he spoke that it was in fact an idyllic village.

"I heard later that one of the broadsheet reporters wondered if the Blair euphoria was the genuine feeling in Trimdon and Sedgefield, and he went through to the bar where in the corner there was this chap with his cloth cap on sitting with his pint – and by then it had got to about one o'clock, so it was probably his second or third.

"This reporter asked him to say honestly what he thought about his MP becoming Labour leader, and the bloke looked up and said: 'He's young, he's intelligent, he seems to have something special, some great ideas for the future, he's a good MP, he'll make an excellent leader of the party and a great PM.'

"And the reporter said: 'Bloody hell, they're all spin doctors round here!'

"And this bloke wasn't even a member of the party."

The three leadership candidates toured the country searching for votes. "At Darlington, I came out of the hall just as John Prescott was coming out, and I said: 'How's it going, John?'," says Burton. "He said: 'Fine, John, Tony's going to win it and I think I'll be deputy.'

"So John knew the situation, and he's been the best supporter any party leader could have. He believes in New Labour, even though people think he puts up with it."

On July 21, Tony Blair was elected Labour leader with a comfortable majority, his 57 per cent share of the vote overwhelming Prescott's 24.1 per cent and Beckett's 18.9 per cent.

He was just 41-years-old, the youngest of Labour's eight post-War leaders. He soon found out that, by 56.5 per cent to 43.5 per cent, Prescott would be his deputy leader.

Burton was present at the Institute of London as the result was announced. "I was sitting a couple of rows behind Cherie and her father and the tears were just running down my cheeks," says Burton. "I'm hopeless at speeches anyway – I've cried through most of Tony's speeches at conference but this particular day it was just impossible.

"I remember afterwards having an interview with Gerry Foley from Tyne Tees Television, and I was on a different planet. This person I'd met all those years ago, who I'd thought had some potential to do some good for the constituency and the Labour Party had become leader – it was just a wonderful feeling.

"I'm not just saying this, but I was so pleased for other people in the constituency – Paul (Trippett) Peter (Brookes) and Phil (Wilson) who had placed their trust in him. And for the people. We'd got him elected easily enough but in those first two or three years we had to sort out the extreme left, the Trades Council, that was trying to take over the constituency."

But with every silver lining there comes a cloud. "More and more work started coming into the office at Myrobella," says Burton. "Life got much busier but, let's be fair, there was never a dull moment.

"I'd never worked professionally for Tony when he was an ordinary MP although I did spend a lot of time with him whenever he was in the constituency, not only at our house and socially but around the area too.

John Burton: The Grit in the Oyster

"As we'd always done, we continued to spend hours, usually into the early morning, discussing how things had to be and could be changed in the party, what needed to be done, in what order the necessary building blocks had to be put in place.

"The minute he became leader of the party, he started work on changing things and that meant he had to be heavily committed to travelling around the country, attending regional meetings and getting to know better all the influential people in the party."

Just three months after being elected leader, Blair strode onto the stage at the Winter Gardens in Blackpool and told the annual conference that he wanted to scrap Clause IV of the party's constitution. It was a surprise, to say the least, and a shock to most.

Clause IV had been written in 1917 and committed the party to "common ownership", or nationalisation. Since 1959, the Labour leadership had accepted that it was out-dated, but no one had dared tackle this historic problem head-on. For decades, the Tories had used it as a stick to beat Labour – but now Blair decided to be brave.

"This clause still talked, virtually, about nationalising the country's top 300 companies, Marks & Spencer and so on," recalls Burton.

"No matter how much people insisted that we would never do that, it was still party policy. It was just absolute suicide, and Tony and I talked about it in all of our deliberations about changing the party.

"Once he became leader, he had the chance to do it. I sat down with him and told him that he had to go round and had to speak about it because one of his greatest skills is his ability to talk to people and those people can then see that he's concerned, he cares, he still believes essentially in the same principles that people in the party have held for years. Changing Clause IV, he knew, would be a vital move forward. He was the first to really get to grips with the matter. John Smith wouldn't have done it. What Tony was saying was: 'How can we go to the electorate with principles which we know most of them don't agree with?' We'd have had to put up with the media, during the next election, reminding us and the voters that our party policy said that we were going to nationalise the likes of Marks & Spencer. Our insistence that we weren't really going to do that would have made no difference at all. As far as they were concerned it was undeniably our party policy. It took guts to do it but Tony dared to attempt to revise the old Clause IV and he won the day."

Following Blair's nationwide tour, 65 per cent of the vote at a special party conference on April 29, 1995, approved the New Labour constitution.

It is seen as the symbolic moment when New Labour cut the apron strings and left old Labour behind. Burton sees it more as the party catching up with the people. "They'd already cut their ties with old Labour by not voting for them, by keeping them in the wilderness for 17 years," he says. "You can still have your socialist beliefs, you can still believe in compassion and caring and helping the poor, this was just a change in how you say things."

Such a frenetic start to Blair's leadership meant that he was away more than ever before from the constituency, which meant a frenetic start for Burton, the newly-appointed political assistant.

"What he desperately needed was a secure constituency where everything was kept on an even keel and that was my task," he says. "I had to meet all the people in the North-East with whom Tony would have had dealings if he hadn't been away.

"I knew the party well in the whole area. I'd been on the regional executive but I'd always thought that, in the north, it was a bit of a waste of time. I don't mean that to sound heartless but we used to have meetings and conferences which passed resolutions that never went anywhere so they were often little more than talking shops. Nevertheless, people met, voiced their feelings and did feel part of a team.

"I also knew a lot of people through my work on the local council and had met even more in the late 1980s when I was chairman attending a lot of functions and events. So when I needed to make the contacts necessary to enable me to do the job effectively it was easy. The councillors I already knew and soon became well-acquainted with people in the various agencies."

When Conservative Prime Minister John Major asked for Parliament to be dissolved in March 1997, the workload at Myrobella was ratcheted up even further. While Blair took his battlebus around the country, Burton was left conducting the local campaign with the national spotlight shining upon him.

"1997 was a most unusual election," says Burton. "I was in charge of local matters, dealing with things from Myrobella, the local office, and, for the first time, I was doing so without our local MP who was, obviously, needed all over the country. But it seemed as if the majority of the world's media, not just British but Japanese, German, Norwegian, American and the rest, had descended on this constituency and all of them wanted interviews for newspapers, magazines, radio and television – and we didn't have an MP to offer them. Tony was on radio and television every day but he wasn't here.

"It was a weird situation in so many ways. We have a very good party structure with the constituency divided up into branches which were, and are, able to run their individual areas. We couldn't take a battlebus around the constituency with John Burton in it. There would have been no point. People could see me any time. They wanted to see Tony but he was here on only a couple of occasions and then on election day itself – and the one thing you don't do on election day is canvass!"

Those first two days in May 1997 passed Burton in a blur. He remembers on election day – May 1 – taking Blair to a presentation to an old party member in Aycliffe, and then onto some business awards at the Flymo lawnmower factory. "Initially, we'd said that Tony couldn't do it because it was election day and it wasn't normal practice," says Burton. "But then I thought that it was for the managing director, my old school friend Phil Fellows, and I couldn't let him down, and so I said: 'To hell with normal practice, we're changing everything, we're New Labour, let's just pop in while we're near Aycliffe'."

Burton also remembers that he was on doorstepping duty on the evening, making sure that the good voters of Trimdon Village had got to the polls.

And then he remembers driving through to Newton Aycliffe and meeting Blair and Cherie, as arranged, on the steps of the leisure centre, with a warm handshake. Blair's Sedgefield count was taking place inside. It was nearing 11 o'clock.

"We were in the old bar outside the counting hall and the results started to come in – Sunderland was always first," says Burton. "Chris Mullin's result in Sunderland South came in and it was about 12 or 13 per cent change in our favour, and the interesting thing was that was what it was all the way through.

"I remember Tony sitting in the corner with the results coming in on the television. He'd been around the hall and had a word with the tellers and some of the other candidates, and when he returned about midnight there must have been 90 results in. They were all inner city seats, and so the whole of the television screen was red and still he said: 'You can't be complacent.'

"I said: 'I think you can allow yourself a little complacency now, Tony.'

"And then he said: 'I hope they've won some seats'."

Burton believes Blair had in mind the 1993 Canadian wipe-out, where the ruling Progressive Conservative party had gone into the election with 157 seats and had come out of it with just one leaving Jean Chrétien's Liberals with 177 seats and a massive majority.

But it happened. In the 1997 General Election in Britain, Blair's Labour won 419 seats and gained the biggest majority, 179, since 1935.

When Burton introduced him as "the next Prime Minister, our own Tony Blair" from the stage at Trimdon Labour Club in the early hours of the morning, Britain's youngest PM since 1812 was greeted with a rapturous reception.

Once the balloons had risen up to the ceiling and the tumultous welcome had died down, Blair spoke for just 15 minutes. He said: "It is you people here who have been my foundation and support all the way through my political career. It was here, in this constituency, that we created New Labour."

Cries of "Yes, Yes" rang around the hot, sweaty hall, as his faithful Sedgefield followers echoed his every word.

"I believe in you, and believe you represent all the best in this country, and the greatest pride I could ever have is to repay that trust one thousandfold." As he finished, people were jumping, crying, and singing, in sheer joy.

He called Burton "a star", and then left. Burton and his wife, Lily, joined a small, select band – Blair and Cherie, Peter Mandelson, Jonathan Powell, Anji Hunter and Alastair Campbell – in a small plane flying south to the capital. Their journey that night can truly be said to have started in Front Street, Trimdon, and ended in Downing Street, London.

"The cabin crew looking after our creature comforts on the flight down from Teesside came round and asked us what we'd like to drink," says Burton. "Taking their lead from Tony, most on board asked for a soft drink but I fancied a Scotch and lemonade so I asked for one and, having lit my pipe, thoroughly enjoyed both. I'd noticed that Anji kept going into the toilet but thought no more of it until she came up to me, leaned forward and sort of hissed at me in a friendly way: 'You bastard Burton! I've been slipping into the loo to have a smoke and I fancied a real drink too. Why couldn't they have asked me after you'd ordered yours?' I enjoyed the flight down."

Besides the sound of the toilet door opening and closing behind Anji Hunter, Blair's personal advisor, there was little other noise in the cabin.

"It was a very weird atmosphere," says Burton. "Everyone was sat in silence. Any conversations were held in whispers. It was as if everyone were trying to come to terms with what they knew was a momentous occasion."

The rest of those travelling to London from the constituency followed in a larger aircraft. Peter Mandelson was on this flight and, being more technologically-advanced than anyone on the new Prime Minister's plane, the election results were coming through on his mobile phone as they were announced. He later remarked to Burton how strange it was to be flying over the constituencies as their results came in and as, in many cases, they changed political colour.

The two plane-loads of Sedgefield people met up outside the Royal Festival Hall where Labour's celebration party was already in full swing.

"When we got there we were split up from Tony and we couldn't get in, and we didn't know that everybody who had been inside had been told to get out to listen to Tony who was going to speak outside," says Burton. "We were with

145

John Burton: The Grit in the Oyster

Jonathan Powell, this really important bloke, and he was saying to the people on the door: 'We want to be in, I'm Jonathan Powell'. Nobody knew who he was so he started running round the hall saying: 'This is John Burton, Tony's agent, let us in.' It was surreal. Here's Tony's chief of staff running round saying he's with me! It still didn't get us in!"

Even from a distance of six years, Burton finds it very emotional to recall that night and that morning. Hearing Blair speak in those early day-break hours was practically a mystical experience for him.

"I remember him standing there, starting to talk, and the dawn and the light came up behind him, and I thought: 'Bloody hell, he's going to walk on the Thames.' It was a wonderful feeling."

But for Burton the blur continued. "After that, the whole world wanted me. Lily and I did GMTV with Tessa Sanderson and Tony Robinson, and I think they'd brought Father John Caden – Tony's old tennis partner – down from Sedgefield...

"And we stayed that night somewhere near the Oratory School...I don't know where...it was a big posh hotel..."

Lily tries to bring the blur into focus: "It had windows overlooking this lovely garden...a very big bathroom...and a four poster bed..."

"And we never used the bed," says Burton. "We didn't get there until eight o'clock in the morning, we had an hour, and then we went back out again, so God knows how much it cost us not to sleep in it..."

Much later that morning, a much more composed Tony Blair had an audience with the Queen at Buckingham Palace, and he accepted her request to him to form a new government. He arrived in Downing Street at 1pm to more cheers from assembled staff and friends.

"It was a moment to remember forever," recalls Burton. "A kind of video of it all runs in my head whenever I look back on it. I hear the applause; I see the television cameras, the outstretched hands holding those pleading microphones; it's all in a weird sort of slow motion. Then, through a sort of haze, Tony goes through the door of Number 10 with his family and the door closes behind him. I'm left outside."

He continues: "I've never told Tony this, but I'm sure he knows that when that door closed, I wondered why I hadn't been invited inside. I don't think that it had occurred to me that I wouldn't be and that I, and the rest of us from the north, would not be allowed to go in. In retrospect, and knowing what I do now, it was never going to happen – but, at the time, it hurt; it hurt like mad. But time's a great healer. Since then, I've always enjoyed an excellent working relationship with Downing Street. They've always respected me and they respect the fact that I've got a special relationship with Tony. Yes, they do tend to want to protect him, look after him, but just now and then they seem to want to lock him, metaphorically, in a cupboard.

"It wasn't Tony's fault that I wasn't invited into Number 10. It wasn't anyone else's either and it wasn't an oversight. Tony Blair, that ambitious young man who had knocked at our front door in Trimdon Village so many years before, had become the political leader of the nation and those who take care of such matters needed to follow precedent and to brief him, as quickly as possible, about national and international matters and protocols."

The incident clearly still rankles with Burton. He diplomatically tries to brush it off, but his feelings were reinforced some years later when he met Philip Gould, the poll and focus group expert who had played a key role in preparing Labour for victory. He too had been shut out of Downing Street at that historic moment, and he too had felt devastated.

However, Burton and the Sedgefield posse quickly recovered their composure by adjourning to the nearest pub to Downing Street where they immediately felt at home: it was the Red Lion in Whitehall, as opposed to the Red Lion in Trimdon.

"This young lad came up to me," says Burton. "He was a big lad with a T-shirt on, in his twenties, and there were tears streaming down his face. He said he wished his father had been alive as he'd longed for a Labour Government.

"Everybody in London was a foot off the ground. A Japanese tourist stopped us and asked for a picture – he'd seen us on television.

"I took Lily to a Hockney exhibition in Bond Street and while we were wandering round someone came up and said: 'Thanks very much, I'm a BBC engineer, thanks for changing everything and giving us a Labour government.' That's when I finally realised what we'd achieved."

Says Lily: "You got out there on the streets, and people were coming up and shaking our hands, saying thank-you for Tony. It was as if the greyness had lifted."

12: A still and quiet conscience

WITH his boss away in Westminster, John Burton has to field the mail, the e-mail and the phone calls that flood into the Sedgefield constituency office.

Some come from the boss himself. "Tony tends to ring me more when he's travelling because then he has a bit of time to be able to do that," says Burton. "Even if we do have little problems up here, I don't want to concern him with every single one of them.

"When he calls, he might ask me what I think people are feeling about certain matters and I tell him. Some of the calls can be amusing for all sorts of reasons. There was one not long ago when there was something wrong with the phone at his end. I could hear a voice but didn't recognise who it was. It was indistinct, so I asked, 'Who's that?' Then I repeated myself more forcefully, 'Who is that?'

"I was just about to put the phone down because I was getting nowhere when a slightly clearer voice said, 'John. John, it's me. Good heavens, it's terrible when your agent doesn't recognise you.' So I had a chat to him and then took the phone over to Lily who hadn't heard my conversation. It was at that point that the problem started again. 'Who are you?' Lily asked, looking at me. The voice at the other end suddenly became clearer. 'Heavens, now even my agent's wife doesn't know who I am. Perhaps I need to come north more often.'"

Burton continues: "Tony puts a lot of trust in me with regard to all constituency matters and I'm lucky to have a lot of friends, like Peter Brookes, Paul Trippett, Terry Ward and a lot of others, including Lucy Hovells, who help me look after the patch. In the office Christine Warbis, Rita Welsh and Lily (Burton) work beyond the call of duty and Mick Hills has also been invaluable.

"I can't mention everybody simply because there's a whole cohort across the entire area and everyone plays his or her part. The job I do has simply got bigger and bigger – but I'm not complaining. I still enjoy every minute. Tony realises the job that these people do. He knows that we can get on and deal with all sorts of problems which arise in any constituency. We deal with regional bodies, with the regional development agency One NorthEast, with all the leaders of all the councils, they all come here."

And many come to Myrobella not expecting to talk to the monkey but demanding the organ-grinder.

"There are people in the constituency, and further afield too, who refuse to believe that Tony's not here all the time," says Burton. "They may have seen him live on television during Prime Minister's Questions in the Commons or at a summit meeting somewhere overseas but they still think that he's also, somehow, here in Trimdon and they telephone and want to speak to him – now!

"But we cope. Tony never underrates the importance of constituency business. Obviously, as Prime Minister, he can't be here as often as he once was but this is still his home as well as his local office.

"When first elected as our MP, he came up almost every week, then it was fortnightly and, of necessity, that interval's been extended to about five weeks. That can't be helped. He's now the British Prime Minister and his constituents are delighted that 'our Tony' has achieved such high office but, to them, he continues to be 'our Tony'. The rest of the country, and the world, address him as 'Prime Minister' but on his home ground, in Sedgefield, he is and always will be just 'Tony'. I think that he'd be very surprised, indeed perturbed, if at one of his regular question and answer sessions in Trimdon Labour Club someone addressed him as 'Prime Minister'.

"When he arrives at Myrobella, one of the first things he does is take off his suit, put on his jeans, shirt or jogging top and trainers; then he sits in the garden with a cup of tea and reads the papers or if it's raining or a bit too cold outside he'll lie on the sofa and watch some old B-movie on the television. One of the best things, to my mind, is that if he just wants to go out and have a quiet pint of beer he can still do that. Local people talk to him, of course, but they respect his privacy. In fact, they guard it quite jealously."

Blair fought his first election as Prime Minister in June 2001, the calling of it having been delayed by the foot-and-mouth epidemic. By a geographical quirk, the Tory leader was William Hague whose North Yorkshire constituency of Richmond bordered Sedgefield along the River Tees to the south of Darlington. The bridge at Croft, where journalists could walk across the watery divide from Blair's village of Hurworth into Hague's North Yorkshire, became the emblem of the campaign.

For Burton, polling day on June 7 broke early as he had been rota'd for the first duty at the polling station in Trimdon Village. He knew, and had a few words for, everyone who came through its doors. Some he had taught at Trimdon or at Sedgefield. He knew all their names and asked after their families; he'd known many for more than half a century.

Later in the morning, he moved on to Myrobella, and watched as Blair and his wife, accompanied by their three eldest children, walked the short distance across the playing fields from Myrobella to their designated polling station to cast their votes. Reporters, photographers and camera crews had massed on specially-erected scaffolding for the photo-opportunity.

Candidate and agent were then driven off to make a few appearances around the constituency, including one at the Constituency Labour Club in Trimdon Village to thank all the party workers.

At lunchtime, John Prescott flew to Myrobella by helicopter, landing on the playing field that the Blairs had earlier walked across. Burton greeted the Deputy Prime Minister and then left the assembled politicians and others so that he could have a quiet sandwich lunch in his own garden with Lily.

After a relatively peaceful afternoon, it was time to put on a new suit, a present from Lily, to carry out his duties as Election Agent and Chairman of Sedgefield Constituency Labour Party. He walked down to the Labour Club ready for a long night both there and at the count at Newton Aycliffe. He was not complacent, just quietly confident about the outcome of the approaching night.

His outlining of the day that his man achieved a record second landslide victory sounds amazingly down-to-earth and matter-of-fact. Perhaps it was because Mr Hague over the water in North Yorkshire was the only person not convinced by Labour's lead in the polls; perhaps it was because the turn-out on the day dropped dis-spiritingly below 60 per cent; perhaps it was because Blair, Burton and the government accepted that their work in office was not even half done.

Yet the Sedgefield faithful did allow themselves a moment of exuberance. "We'd been over the moon with the result in 1997," says Burton, "but this was another Labour milestone. We were so very proud of our MP and his tremendous achievement. When, after the count, he walked into Trimdon Labour Club, his reception was no less rapturous than it had been four years earlier."

Towards the end of 2002 and at the start of 2003, as the war clouds over Iraq grew darker, Burton noticed that the volume of post coming into Myrobella fell. The flood of e-mails and phone calls turned into more of a steady trickle.

"It seemed," he says, "as if people realised that Tony had a lot on his plate, especially with regard to Iraq. In fact, a lot of people got in touch just to ask how he was and to send messages of support for what he was trying to do. Some others contacted us to express their concerns about or opposition to his actions and that's no more nor less than we expected."

Naturally enough, Blair was regularly on the phone asking what Burton's antennae were picking up.

"I told him that it seemed to a lot of people as if he was rather out on his own on this one," he says. "I told him that the easiest thing for him to do was nothing. I told him that nobody likes Saddam Hussein but nobody particularly wants to go to war over him.

"I said that if Bill Clinton had been the American president, there would have been no problem, but it was George Bush and it was seen as if Tony was allying himself to a right-wing conspiracy.

"And he replied without hesitation, and I realised how he had grown over the years. He said: 'Doing nothing is not an option, John. For our children and grandchildren's sake we must get rid of this man. Not only has he had weapons of mass destruction but he is involved with the cells of terrorists. Doing nothing is not an option. We have to do something.' And that was that."

The media came to Sedgefield to find out how the war was playing with Blair's own constituents apparently in the belief that many were totally against his actions.

"But they weren't," Burton asserts. "The vast majority were 100 per cent behind him. They didn't have a problem with the course of action on which he'd embarked. They didn't have any detailed information as to why he was doing what he was doing but they believed that if he was doing it then he must have a very good reason for doing so. In other words they believed him and they backed him.

"There was a faction, the Sedgefield Against The War thing, which started off with about a hundred people but ended with few more than a half dozen on a Saturday morning standing outside on the green.

"I believe the people stood firmly behind him because they respect him, they have confidence in his judgement, they like him and they support him – they really do."

So although there was a loud anti-war hubbub, Burton regularly transmitted to Blair that he had more support than he might imagine if he solely listened to the voices of the media.

"I always said to him that there was a big and supportive silent majority out there, the people who don't say anything," says Burton. "To some extent, it was the more 'involved' people who, even if they're just on the fringe of politics, voice their opinions, and it turned out that way."

On March 19, 2003, Parliament debated whether Britain should go to war against Iraq with the United States but without specific United Nations support. It was a day of high political drama played out against the backdrop of a large backbench Labour rebellion, the size of which would determine whether Blair could continue in office.

"If he'd been defeated on that vote, he would have resigned," says Burton. "He told me that he wouldn't go back to the House for a vote of confidence, he'd just go.

"Bush was aware of this, and he phoned Tony and said: 'Don't think you have to commit yourself to the point where you lose everything. I will do it alone.'

"That was massive for Bush, and Tony said: 'Hey, if you believe something, are committed to something, you can't change your mind. I can't say that we'll go to war today but not tomorrow if the only reason for the change is that I might not be Prime Minister.'

"Tony was prepared to go to those lengths of losing everything, so sure was he that he was right in what he was doing."

The day began with two junior ministers following the path trodden by Robin Cook, the leader of the House of Commons and former Foreign Secretary, in resigning.

Blair rose to speak at 12.30pm. He appeared to have shaken off the virus which had dogged him for weeks, making him look tired and haggard, and which had been the subject of almost as much media attention as his motives for going to war.

His impassioned speech lasted 60 minutes and was, quite possibly, his finest hour in the House since Sedgefield had first elected him in 1983. He concluded: "If this House now demands that at this moment, faced with this threat from this regime, that British troops are pulled back, that we turn away at the point of reckoning – and that is what it means – what then?

"What will Saddam feel? Strengthened beyond measure. What will the other states who tyrannise their people, the terrorists who threaten our existence, what will they take from that? That the will confronting them is decaying and feeble.

"This is not the time to falter. It is time for this House to give a lead, to show that we will stand up for what we know to be right."

It was enough. In the end, 139 MPs voted against the Government – barely enough to embarrass the Prime Minister.

"Before that vote," says Burton, "there were people who were accusing Tony of sitting on the fence, listening to public opinion polls and spin doctors. After it, they could no longer level that accusation at him.

"My estimation of the man has always been extremely high but, if it's possible, after that vote it went even higher, essentially because of the strength of character he showed. At the same time, I was worried because I knew that we had a great prime minister who still had a lot to do, who was still trying to turn the National Health Service round, was still working on Third World issues, wanted to do so much more for education and for law and order. I was worried that he would have felt he had to go because of this one, admittedly enormous, policy matter but he was unshakeably convinced that he was doing the right thing and that it was the correct thing for the country to do."

To Burton, the potential loss of Blair would have been catastrophic for country and party.

"I was recently part of a robust discussion during which it was pointed out just how radical Blair's Government has been," he says. "Some trade union officials were having a go at it and our Constituency Labour Party trade union liaison officer, Vince Crosby from the Transport and General Workers, suggested that instead of 'chuntering on' about going back to the old days, they should remember that this Government has introduced 500 measures which affect the trade unions – 500! He wasn't talking just about the minimum wage and the working families tax credit, rather all the things like the right to statutory holidays, and not just union related matters but others such as the reform of the House of Lords. These are things that Clem Attlee didn't do, Harold Wilson didn't do; they didn't dare. But this Government's done it.

"Now I grant you that not everything's yet the way that everybody wants it. The reform of the Lords will go further, I'm sure. But, nevertheless, this Government's done a heck of a lot and I'm sure that Tony Blair will eventually go down as not only a great prime minister but as a very radical one as well. The changes in the health service are fundamental as is the principle that schools should have more control of their own money and more say in how they're financed.

"So many things have changed or are changing. It's quite amazing and yet the Government's never praised for what it does, which is a shame really. When people talk to me about returning to the old days, I always give the same answer: 'The old days? Wasn't that when we were in opposition?'.

"I suppose that some people feel more comfortable with the notion of opposition. You can say what you like and don't have any real responsibilities but then you don't and can't do anything for the very people you're trying to represent."

As the war – although not its aftermath – came to an end, thoughts in Sedgefield and Downing Street turned to commemorating the 20th anniversary of Blair's election as an MP.

"Some time earlier, Cherie had made it quite clear that she didn't want 'a big, posh do'," recalls Burton. "There had been suggestions that some of the biggest names in show business, and I mean the biggest names, could be invited to entertain at the event at some prestigious venue and that tickets should be £100 each. Now, come on! In this area, that would have been a joke.

"Cherie insisted that it had to be 'local', with friends, and that it had to be in Trimdon Labour Club. Now you have to agree: what more prestigious venue could you want? Most of the significant happenings in Tony's 20 years have happened or have been celebrated there."

Having decided upon the venue, the discussion turned to the evening's musical entertainment.

"Cherie said that she wanted the music to be provided by local groups," says Burton. "She and Tony have heard Skerne, the folk band in which I play, dozens of times, so we were invited to perform. Reg Walls' New Orleans Jazz Band had to be there and Habit, my son Jonathan's new rock group, also did its bit. Folk, jazz and rock – something for everybody.

"Then came the big question: 'Can we persuade Tony to play?'. Jonathan practised two Free numbers because we knew that Tony liked Free but it was then decided that he might be happier performing with people of about his own age, from his own era or older, as it were."

At 5pm in the club, the Sedgefield supergroup gathered for its one and only practice. It lasted no more than ten minutes.

"David Triesman, General Secretary of the Labour Party since 2001, was there along with Tony," says Burton. "Then there was me on banjo, Peter Brookes and David Hill, lead singer, the man who replaced Alastair Campbell in charge of the party's communications later in the year.

"The practice was a scream. As we were taking out our instruments, I said to David Triesman: 'That looks like a nice guitar.'

"'Yes,' he said, 'I bought it from Jeff Beck. It's the one he used on Hey Ho Silver Lining. It's not one of my most favourite songs but it is a very good guitar.'

"Tony produced a white Fender Stratocaster, with a rose motif on it, which he had acquired from Bryan Adams, and the bass player for the session was from our young rock group. He did remarkably well."

Skerne opened the show, their set only slightly up-staged by Blair's arrival and his progress through the hall, his every move and handshake followed by the cameras.

"Throughout the evening, everybody remarked what a really friendly event it was," says Burton. "People were there who'd helped Tony 20 years before but hadn't been with him for the past ten years or so and yet, as he went around, he knew everybody by their first names.

"The atmosphere was wonderful and it was so nice. Cabinet colleagues also came along – Hilary Armstrong, Stephen Byers and Alan Milburn – as did the long-standing MP for Bishop Auckland and former Labour chief whip, Derek Foster. Tony was totally relaxed as were Cherie and the children. The cameras captured what he said in his speech, words which really were from the heart."

After Blair's address, all the pressmen and photographers were sent home, and sometime after 10pm the Sedgefield Supergroup took to the stage.

They performed three classic numbers – Johnny Be Good, Rave On and Midnight Special – and no one embarrassed themselves.

"I don't think we gave a bad performance and, afterwards, I told all the musicians that if we ever had to give up our day jobs we could buy a battered old van and take to the road," says Burton. "None of them were very interested.

"But I think we sounded like a proper rock band on the stage and then, as well, afterwards because Tony came up to me and said: 'Didn't we play Johnny Be Good in the wrong key?'

"I said: 'Yes, we played it in E because I thought that would be best for David Triesman's voice as he was the only one who knew the lyrics.'

"And Tony said: 'Well, I could have sung it in G!' It turned out that he not only knew the correct key but all the words as well. If I'd known before we went on, I'd have let him sing it."

Over the years, Burton's life has not become busier just because of his increased responsibility for the constituency office. He has taken on other roles such as accepting an invitation to be a member of the Council of Durham Cathedral.

"To me it's more than a great honour to be part of that group," he says. "The cathedral's played such an important part in my life that I hope I can now give something back to it by serving on that body. I remember vividly being taken there as a child and now Lily and I take our grandson, Rikki-Lee, there. I really believe that it's the finest building in the world and I'll always stand by that statement because, in my experience, and I have travelled a bit, it's unmatched in so many ways."

He is also now a Deputy Lieutenant of County Durham, his name having being put forward, he thinks, because of his years of work for the community and for sport. "I'm one of a number of people who can stand in for the Lord Lieutenant should the need arise. Again, it's an honour and one which I appreciate very much."

He says that he will carry on with his constituency role for as long as Blair needs him. Before anyone can draw any inference from that about how long the Prime Minister will continue, the agent is quick to add that neither of them is so much as beginning to contemplate the start of giving up for some time yet, even though they have been working together for 20 years.

"When I look back across those years which teamed me, and others, with a political aspirant who went on to become the Prime Minister of Great Britain, I sometimes wonder where the time went," says Burton.

"To quote William Shakespeare, it's 'such stuff as dreams are made on'. With hindsight, I would change barely a single second of those 20 years. Tony and I have been the firmest of friends throughout that time and I can't see how anything or anyone could ever change that.

"I didn't make Tony Blair Prime Minister of Great Britain. I may have given him a helping hand along the way but that's for history, not for me, to decide."